PEOPLE OF THE STATE OF CALIFORNIA v. PHILLIP SPECTOR

Case File

ASPEN PUBLISHERS

PEOPLE OF THE STATE OF CALIFORNIA v. PHILLIP SPECTOR

Case File

ANN M. MURPHY

Associate Professor
Gonzaga University School of Law

Wolters Kluwer
Law & Business

AUSTIN   BOSTON   CHICAGO   NEW YORK   THE NETHERLANDS

To contact Customer Care, e-mail customer.service@aspenpublishers.com,
call 1-800-234-1660, fax 1-800-901-9075, or mail correspondence to:

>Aspen Publishers
>Attn: Order Department
>PO Box 990
>Frederick, MD 21705

Printed in the United States of America.

1 2 3 4 5 6 7 8 9 0

ISBN 978-07355-9795-2

Library of Congress Cataloging-in-Publication Data

Murphy, Ann M., 1958-
    People of the State of California v. Phillip Spector : case file / Ann M. Murphy.
        p. cm.
    Includes index.
    ISBN 978-0-7355-9795-2
1. Evidence, Criminal — United States — Examinations, questions, etc. 2. Trials
(Murder) — California — Alhambra. I. Title.
    KF9660.M87 2010
    345.73′06 — dc22

                                                                    2010019265

About Wolters Kluwer Law & Business

Wolters Kluwer Law & Business is a leading provider of research information and workflow solutions in key specialty areas. The strengths of the individual brands of Aspen Publishers, CCH, Kluwer Law International and Loislaw are aligned within Wolters Kluwer Law & Business to provide comprehensive, in-depth solutions and expert-authored content for the legal, professional and education markets.

CCH was founded in 1913 and has served more than four generations of business professionals and their clients. The CCH products in the Wolters Kluwer Law & Business group are highly regarded electronic and print resources for legal, securities, antitrust and trade regulation, government contracting, banking, pension, payroll, employment and labor, and healthcare reimbursement and compliance professionals.

Aspen Publishers is a leading information provider for attorneys, business professionals and law students. Written by preeminent authorities, Aspen products offer analytical and practical information in a range of specialty practice areas from securities law and intellectual property to mergers and acquisitions and pension/benefits. Aspen's trusted legal education resources provide professors and students with high-quality, up-to-date and effective resources for successful instruction and study in all areas of the law.

Kluwer Law International supplies the global business community with comprehensive English-language international legal information. Legal practitioners, corporate counsel and business executives around the world rely on the Kluwer Law International journals, loose-leafs, books and electronic products for authoritative information in many areas of international legal practice.

Loislaw is a premier provider of digitized legal content to small law firm practitioners of various specializations. Loislaw provides attorneys with the ability to quickly and efficiently find the necessary legal information they need, when and where they need it, by facilitating access to primary law as well as state-specific law, records, forms and treatises.

Wolters Kluwer Law & Business, a unit of Wolters Kluwer, is headquartered in New York and Riverwoods, Illinois. Wolters Kluwer is a leading multinational publisher and information services company.

For my father
The kindest person I've ever known

CONTENTS

PREFACE

Oddly enough, the idea for this book took root in the People's Republic of China. I was a Fulbright Lecturer in Beijing teaching at the Central University of Finance and Economics (CUFE) in 2007 and 2008 and was asked to teach American Evidence. The jury system is quite rare in the world, and there is no jury system in China. It is a civil law country (as opposed to the United States, which is a common law country) and there were no uniform rules of evidence. I considered how I would teach Chinese students the Federal Rules of Evidence. How would they be able to comprehend that we purposely do not tell the jury certain things — a lot of things. Using an actual case seemed like a good plan. I went about searching for an interesting case and found *People of the State of California v. Phillip Spector*. It proved to be an excellent teaching tool. My students even had a Moot Court exercise based upon the case. The students were absolutely amazing in their opening statements, direct and cross-examination of witnesses, and closing arguments, which they did in English, a foreign language for them.

With the new focus on "realistic training" in law schools suggested by the Carnegie Foundation for the Advancement of Teaching, I have attempted to structure this book with a heavy emphasis on the practical skills needed by future lawyers.

I am indebted to many people for making this book possible. First, I must acknowledge the victim, Lana Clarkson, who was a beautiful actress who died violently far too early. The defendant, Phil Spector, apparently struggled with mental demons most of his life and now sits in a California detention facility. There is no good news here, except that students may benefit from the learning experience. Thank you to CUFE and its students for giving me the inspiration for this book.

I am extremely grateful to Los Angeles County Superior Court Judge Larry Paul Fidler, Assistant District Attorney Alan Jackson, and attorney Doron Weinberg. Thanks as well to Professor Laurie L. Levenson, brand-new California attorney Deborah Morse, Public Information Officer Sandi Gibbons, and Betsy Ross.

I could not have tackled this case without the help of my research assistant (now both a Washington state and California state lawyer) Linda Currey, research assistant Alena Wolotira, assistant Vicky Daniels, and Gonzaga University School of Law.

And of course, thanks to my husband and children for enduring seemingly endless nights without me.

THE MURDER

SUPERIOR COURT OF THE STATE OF CALIFORNIA
FOR THE COUNTY OF LOS ANGELES

The People of the State of California,	
Plaintiff,	CASE NO. BA255233
v.	
PHILLIP SPECTOR	INDICTMENT

Criminal Case

Victim: LANA CLARKSON, actress (*Fast Times at Ridgemont High, Barbarian Queen*) and door security (VIP Hostess) at the Foundation Room, House of Blues, Sunset Strip. Age 40.

Defendant: PHILLIP SPECTOR, famous record producer (Ike and Tina Turner, The Righteous Brothers, The Ronettes, The Beatles, The Ramones) known for the "Wall of Sound" technique. Inducted into the Rock and Roll Hall of Fame 1989. Age 63.

Location: "The Pyrenees Castle" — 1700 Grandview Drive, Alhambra (County of Los Angeles), California. Phil Spector's home. Previously a 28-room hotel.

Charges: Indicted September 20, 2004 (Felony Complaint, District Attorney of Los Angeles, November 18, 2003). Unsealed September 27, 2004.

Result of Jury Trial #1: Trial began April 25, 2007. State called 42 witnesses and defense called 35 witnesses. Jury deadlocked (10-2 in favor of conviction). Judge declared mistrial September 26, 2007.

Result of Jury Trial #2: Trial began October 29, 2008. State called 36 witnesses and defense called 18 witnesses. Verdict April 13, 2009. Guilty of second-degree murder. Also found guilty of illegally discharging a firearm.

Sentenced: Nineteen years to life (fifteen years to life for second-degree murder and four years for the personal use of the gun that killed Clarkson), May 29, 2009. Also ordered to pay $16,800 in funeral expenses and $9,740 to the State's Victim's Restitution Fund. Housed at California Substance Abuse Treatment Facility and State Prison, Corcoran, California.

Appeal: Filed California Court of Appeal, Second Appellate District — Division Three (case number B216425) on June 1, 2009. Opening Brief for the Appellant Spector filed March 10, 2010. Government brief due June 8, 2010.

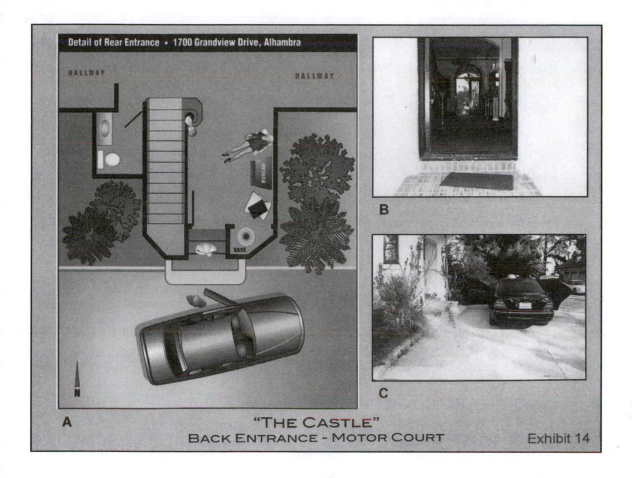

Detail of Rear Entrance • 1700 Grandview Drive, Alhambra

HALLWAY   HALLWAY

VASE

N

A

B

C

"THE CASTLE"
BACK ENTRANCE - MOTOR COURT

Exhibit 14

In his appellate brief filed in March of 2010, Mr. Spector alleges the following:

1. Judge Fidler made "testimonial" statements at Mr. Spector's second trial and these statements violated Mr. Spector's Sixth Amendment right to confront witnesses against him;

2. the admission of "prior bad acts" (uncharged brandishing offenses) and Judge Fidler's instructions to the jury on these prior bad acts violated both State of California and federal law;

3. the admission of retired New York police officer Vincent Tannazzo's testimony about a "prior bad act" was reversible error; and

4. the prosecution's misconduct in Deputy District Attorney Do's and Jackson's closing argument (about the amount of fees charged by Mr. Spector's experts) violated Mr. Spector's due process rights.

SUPERIOR COURT OF THE STATE OF CALIFORNIA
FOR THE COUNTY OF LOS ANGELES

DONNA CLARKSON,

Plaintiff,

v.

PHIL SPECTOR

CASE NO. GC034858

Civil Case

Civil Case: Donna Clarkson, individually, and as Successor in Interest to *Lana Clarkson v. Phil Spector, et al.* Filed February 2, 2005. Pending. Wrongful Death; Survival Action: Negligence; Survival Action: Battery.

Related Cases:

> *Phillip Spector v. Robert L. Shapiro, et al.* Case No. BC317958. Filed July 1, 2004. Breach of Fiduciary Duty; Conversion; Constructive Fraud; Unjust Enrichment; Claim and Delivery; Money Had and Received; Constructive Trust; Rescission and Restitution; and Declaratory Relief. Dismissed without prejudice, December 2005. Refiled December 19, 2007.
>
> *Bonaventure Hotel & Suites Los Angeles v. Phil and Rachelle Spector*, filed June 18, 2008, for unpaid bills.
>
> *Phil Spector v. Michelle Blaine*, filed September 2005, settled for $900,000 in Mr. Spector's favor, October 2006.
>
> *Caplan v. Superior Court of Los Angeles*, filed June 25, 2007, BA255233. Petition Summarily Denied by Order on Appeal, Second Appellate District, Division Three, Case Number B200026.

"I Think My Boss Killed Somebody"

At approximately 5:05 A.M. on the morning of Monday, February 3, 2003, Adriano DeSouza dialed 911 to the Alhambra, California Police Department and stated, "Hi. It's a — my name is Adriano. I'm, uh, Phil, Phil Spector driver. I think my boss killed somebody. Please can, can you send the, uh, uh, a car — "

Police Officers Respond

Alhambra Police Officers Mike Page, Efren Tamayo, Bea Rodriguez, Brandon Cardella, James Hammond, and other officers initially responded to the 911 call.

The radio call indicated that shots were fired and that a reporting party (later determined to be DeSouza) indicated he had seen his boss with a gun in his hand and that he had shot a woman inside the castle. The address given was a large home in Alhambra, California.

Officer Bea Rodriguez arrived at the security gate at 1700 Grandview Drive and spoke to Adriano DeSouza. He told her that he had heard one gunshot, saw a body on the floor with blood on her head, and that Phil Spector had said to him "I think I killed her." According to the police reports, five officers of the Alhambra Police Department approached the castle. A black Mercedes limousine was located in the driveway.

One of the officers saw movement on the second floor of the residence. A few seconds later, Phil Spector suddenly appeared at the rear door of the residence and the officers gave him verbal commands to remain still and remove his hands from his pockets. He was dressed in a black shirt and black pants. Spector removed his hands from his pockets and held them up in the air for approximately three seconds, then he went back inside the residence. The officers yelled for him to exit the castle and to put his hands up. He came outside of the residence again, then he went back inside. According to Officer Page, Mr. Spector said "you've got to come in and see this."

This time the officers followed him into the castle, and Corporal Page shot him twice with an M26 Air Taser. One of the Taser darts hit his upper chest area, and the other dart hit near the lower part of his body. Officer Page reported that Mr. Spector "showed no visible signs of incapacitation." Because he did not react to the Taser shots, Officer Cardella rushed him with a ballistic shield and Corporal Page activated the Air Taser again against Spector's chest. Again, Officer Page reported that he saw "no visible signs of incapacitation." Corporal Page and Hammond wrestled him to the ground. The Air Taser was activated again, but it missed Spector and hit the ground.

While Officers Page and Cardella were attempting to handcuff Mr. Spector, Officer Page became concerned that Mr. Spector could reach his Taser gun. He discarded it to his right. He was also concerned that Mr. Spector could reach his service revolver, so he yelled to Officer Cardella to remove it from his body. He asked Officer Hammond to help to secure Mr. Spector. Mr. Spector was placed in handcuffs.

Officer Page reported that he then looked to the victim and saw that she appeared to be lifeless. He saw a small black revolver near her left ankle. He indicated that it had blood on its wood grips.

Officer Rodriguez reported that she heard Mr. Spector say "What's wrong with you guys?" and "What are you doing?" Later she reportedly heard him say "I didn't mean to shoot her, it was an accident," and "I have an explanation for this."

The Tape Recording at the Scene

Officer Page turned on a microcassette recorder that he had in the pocket of his uniform. A transcript of the recording contained the following statements of Mr. Spector:

- I'm not Robert Blake
- What the hell is wrong with you?
- Oh, what the f*** is wrong with you?
- What are you worried about?
- God, LAPD works for me.
- I can tell you what happened
- You're acting stupid
- Get the f*** off of me
- I'm sorry there's a dead woman here. But I'm sorry but this happened. I can explain it but if you'd just give me a chance.
- What the hell are you acting like ass****s?
- Why are you standing on my head, ass****?
- The Chief of Police worked for me. If you want me to call him, I'll call him. I don't want to be an ass****. I'm sorry this happened. I don't know how it happened, but it happened and I'm sorry this happened.
- The gun went off accidently. She works at the House of Blues. It was a mistake.
- Oh God, I'm just gonna go to sleep. Would you like me to go to sleep?
- I don't know how it happened. It scared the s*** out of me that happened.
- When I see the damage that's been done — this is the most devastating thing I've ever seen in my life.

Mr. Spector Was Arrested at 6:09 A.M.

He was transported to the Alhambra Police Department by another officer, Officer Heckers.

The microcassette recorder was removed from the stairs by Corporal Juarez. Officer Page was given the recorder. The tape was missing and Corporal Juarez indicated he had given it to Officer Kennedy. Officer Page returned to the Alhambra Police Department and was told that Officer Kennedy still had the tape. He returned to Mr. Spector's residence and retrieved the tape. He listened to the tape. Officer Page later gave it to Los Angeles Detectives Fournier and Tomlin at 1:15 P.M.

The Victim

The victim was found slumped in a chair in the foyer of the living room. Officer Cardella checked for any signs of life, and found none. She was wearing a black slipdress, black nylons and black shoes. She had a leopard print purse slung over her right shoulder. She had a single-entry gunshot wound to the mouth. Broken teeth were found scattered around her. A gun was found by the victim's left leg. It was a Colt, 2-inch, blue steel, .38 caliber, six shot revolver. The weapon had five live cartridges in the cylinder and one spent cartridge under the hammer of the gun. Paramedics arrived at the Pyrenees Castle and pronounced the victim (later determined to be Lana Clarkson) dead at 6:24 A.M.

The Initial Evidence

The police reported that they found the following at Phil Spector's home that morning:

- Blood smears on the back door handle
- Blood smears on the stairway railing
- A lever for a dead bolt lock on the back door (lying on the floor)
- Men's (sic) white coat — blood smear on the sleeve and blood spatters on the lapel
- Blood soaked cloth (diaper)
- Brandy glass partially filled with alcohol
- Jose Cuervo tequila bottle
- Partially empty Canada Dry soft drink

Adriano DeSouza

Adriano DeSouza was Phil Spector's driver and had been employed for four months by Mr. Spector. He was interviewed at the scene by Officers Kennedy and Rodriguez. He said that he thought the woman's name was "Lana" or "Lena." He said that he had dropped Mr. Spector and the victim off at the front of the castle. He next saw Mr. Spector approximately 30 minutes after that when he gave Mr. Spector his leather bag, cell phone, and portable DVD player at the back door of the castle. He said he later heard a gunshot and then saw Mr. Spector open the rear door holding a handgun. When he looked inside the house, he saw the victim in a chair with blood on her face. Mr. DeSouza asked Mr. Spector "what happened, sir?"

He indicated that Spector said "I think I killed somebody." He reported that Mr. Spector had the gun in his right hand and indicated it was a black revolver. He told the police officers that Mr. Spector was "completely drunk."

Mr. DeSouza stated that he drove himself away from the residence in the black Mercedes Benz. First he called Mr. Spector's secretary Michelle Blaine, then he called 911. He stayed on the line until the Alhambra police arrived. Officer Rodriguez transported Mr. DeSouza to the Alhambra Police Department at 6:50 A.M.

Earlier That Evening (Evening of February 2, 2003)

On the evening of February 2, 2003, Mr. DeSouza had driven Mr. Spector to four restaurants and bars — The Grill Restaurant and Trader Vic's in Beverly Hills; and Dan Tana's Restaurant and The House of Blues in West Hollywood. Ms. Clarkson was employed at the House of Blues as "door security" for the Foundation Room, a special room at the House of Blues for VIPs. Her shift ran from 6:00 P.M. to 2:00 A.M. She was told by her supervisor to treat Mr. Spector "like Dan Ackroyd — like gold." At The House of Blues, Mr. Spector had ordered an $8.50 alcoholic drink, a $5 bottle of water, and left a $450.00 tip. He paid with a Diner's Club charge card. Ms. Clarkson clocked out of work at 2:21 A.M. and a witness saw Mr. Spector and Ms. Clarkson leave the House of Blues together. Mr. Spector was wearing a white jacket, black shirt, and black pants.

At the Alhambra Police Department (Morning of February 3, 2003)

Officer Derek Gilliam observed and talked with Mr. Spector at the Alhambra jail. He described Mr. Spector as very belligerent and angry. According to Officer Gilliam, Mr. Spector began calling the jailor a "fat ass." Mr. Spector reportedly kept asking whether the police department planned to do anything about the dead lady at his residence. He described Mr. Spector as being uncooperative. When he was photographed at the station, he became more and more belligerent. Officer Gilliam indicated that Mr. Spector smelled of alcohol and he slurred his words. He stated in his police report that Mr. Spector looked at him with a blank stare and asked him what happened at his house.

While speaking with Officer Gilliam, Mr. Spector stated, "I don't know where she got the gun from but she started waiving it around." He then indicated that she began singing his songs (songs he produced) and she stuck the gun to her head and pulled the trigger. The following is from Officer Gilliam's police report:

> During this time he was telling me about the victim and her actions, he was extremely animated with his actions. Spector took his right hand and formed it into a gun by folding his three lower fingers (pinky to middle finger) pointing his index finger straight out, and holding his thumb in a manner which reflects the hammer of a gun. He would put it to the right side of his head and move his thumb in the same manner that a hammer on a gun would move. When he would pretend to pull the trigger he showed me the way her head went back and how she wouldn't move. A couple of times he would hold the position of his head on the back of the chair for approx. 5-10 seconds. I was a little concerned because each time he performed the scenario it was done with more and more emotion and he would hold his head back longer. During one of the demonstrations he looked at me, smirked and said "you don't pull a gun on me" and did a slight giggle.

Mr. Spector refused to take a breathalyzer test.

Michelle Blaine (Mr. Spector's then-assistant) came to the front counter of the Alhambra Police Department (along with Jay Romaine). Rommie Davis, who identified herself as a friend of Mr. Spector's, called the Police Department and indicated that she wanted to speak with Mr. Spector.

Officer Rodriguez saw Mr. Spector at approximately 11:43 A.M. She reported that he "displayed symptoms of intoxication. He emitted the odor of an alcoholic beverage from his breath and person (he was now wearing a tan jail shirt and tan jail pants). I noticed that his eyes were bloodshot and watery." She began to record a conversation between Mr. Spector and Detective Pineda. The following is part of that conversation:

Det. Pineda: Okay, well, you're being charged with murder.
Spector: I'm being charged with murder?
Det. Pineda: Yes. That's one of the things that *****
Spector: Of whom?
Det. Pineda: Okay, well — I don't have her name yet, but . . . um . . . Have you contacted your attorney?
Spector: No. I haven't been allowed to do a damn thing. That's why I wanted to talk to —
Det. Pineda: Okay.
Spector: — uh, Jay and Michelle.

• • •

Det. Pineda: Okay. But you wanna speak to Jay Romaine, right? That's his name?

Spector: Yeah.

Det. Pineda: Okay. Because there's a Romy, but she's a — she's a woman?

Spector: Romy was the person I wanted to call who was trying to reach Robert Shapiro.

• • •

Det. Pineda: But you were — you were arrested for . . . murder.

Spector: Well, of whom?

Det. Pineda: Okay. Well, that's — that's one thing we wanna figure out. Um —

Spector: This is the most bizarre nonsense, and this is absurd.

Det. Pineda: Oh —

Spector: This is absolutely absurd.

Det. Pineda: Okay. Well let me make arrangements — You wanna get a hold of your . . . Is Robert Shapiro gonna be your attorney?

Spector: Yes.

• • •

Spector: I want him down here. I'm gonna make you f***ing people pay for this. This is bull****.

• • •

Spector: This is nonsense. You people have had me here six f***ing hours, maybe nine hours. And you have me locked up like some Goddamn f***ing turd, in some f***ing piece of s***. And you treat me — and then while this person eats and s***s and farts. And you have me jerking around. And when somebody comes over to my f***ing house who pretends to be security at the House of Blues and comes over to my house — remember . . . I own the House of Blues. Where this lady pretended to work, okay? And then just blows her f***ing head open in my f***ing house. And then comes — and then — and then you people come around and — and arrest me and bang the s*** out of my f***ing ass, and beat the s*** out of me and and then you pretend and arrest me. And then pretend like you're f***ing Alhambra.

And the — the Mayor of Alhambra wants me to have Bono come and sing at the anniversary of — bulls***. This is nonsense. This is absolute f***ing nonsense.

I don't know what the f***ing lady — what her problem is, but she wasn't a security at the House of Blues And she's a piece of s***. And I don't know what her f***ing problem was, but she certainly had no right to come to my f***ing castle, blow her f***ing head open, and *** a murder. What the f*** is wrong with you people?

• • •

Spector: Yeah. I'll tell you what I'm gonna do. I'm going to be f***ing — somebody's gonna pay for the f***ing — I've been locked up for the f***ing last twelve f***ing hours. And you f***ing people come in my house and you rummage through my f***ing house, and you tie me down like a f***ing pig, and you know, while somebody's dying there. And, you know, and — and — and — and it scared the s*** out of everybody — while somebody commits suicide. . . .

At 12:30 P.M., attorney Robert Shapiro arrived at the Alhambra Police Department. Mr. Spector was released on bail at 7:00 P.M. on February 3, 2003.

On September 20, 2004, a State of California Grand Jury indicted Phillip Spector of murder in violation of California Penal Code Section 187(a). On November 18, 2003, the District Attorney of Los Angeles County issued a felony complaint. There also was a special allegation of California Penal Code Section 12022.5(a) the *use of a handgun* in the commission of the offense.

The following are the provisions of the *California Penal Code* provided for in the indictment:

> 187(a) Murder is the unlawful killing of a human being, or a fetus, with malice aforethought.
> 188. Every person guilty of murder in the second degree shall be punished by imprisonment in the state prison for a term of 15 years to life.
> 12022.5(a) Except as provided in subdivision (b), any person who personally uses a firearm in the commission of a felony or attempted felony shall be punished by an additional and consecutive term of imprisonment in the state prison for 3, 4, or 10 years, unless use of a firearm is an element of that offense.

On April 13, 2009, the foreperson of the jury signed the following guilty verdict:

> We, the jury in the above-entitled action, find the defendant PHILLIP SPECTOR, GUILTY of the crime of SECOND DEGREE MURDER of LANA CLARKSON, in violation of Penal Code Section 187(a), a felony, as charged in Count 1 of the Indictment.
>
> We further find the allegation that in the commission of the above offense, said defendant PHILLIP SPECTOR, personally used a firearm, to wit: handgun, within the meaning of Penal Code Section 12022.5(a)(1) to be True.

From the Opening Statements

State of California: "The evidence is going to paint a picture of a man who on February 3, 2003, put a loaded pistol in Lana Clarkson's mouth, inside her mouth, and shot her to death."

Defense: "The science will tell you, through the evidence of science, that Phillip Spector did not shoot Lana Clarkson, the decedent, that he did not hold the gun, and that he did not pull the trigger."

SUPERIOR COURT OF THE STATE OF CALIFORNIA
FOR THE COUNTY OF LOS ANGELES

SECRET

The People of the State of California, Plaintiff, v. **PHILLIP SPECTOR**	CASE NO. **BA255233** INDICTMENT

COUNT 1

The said **PHILLIP SPECTOR** is accused by the Grand Jury of the County of Los Angeles, State of California, by this Indictment, of the crime of **MURDER,** in violation of **Penal Code Section 187(a),** a Felony, committed prior to the finding of this Indictment, and as follows:

On or about February 3, 2003, in the County of Los Angeles, the said **PHILLIP SPECTOR** did unlawfully, and with malice aforethought murder **Lana Clarkson,** a human being.

"NOTICE: The above offense is a serious felony within the meaning of Penal Code Section 1192.7(c)."

"NOTICE: Conviction of this offense will require you to provide specimens and samples pursuant to Penal Code section 296. Willful refusal to provide the specimens and samples is a crime."

A TRUE BILL

_____
Foreperson of the Grand Jury

Presented by the Foreperson of the Grand Jury in the presence of the Grand Jury, in open Superior Court of the State of California, within and for the County of Los Angeles, and filed as a record in said Court this 20th day of September, 2004

JOHN A. CLARKE, Executive Officer/Clerk

By_____
Deputy

STEVE COOLEY, District Attorney

By_____
Deputy

Bail Recommended

$_____

Bail

$ 1,000,000

It is further alleged as to Count 1 that said defendant **PHILLIP SPECTOR** personally used a firearm, a **Handgun,** within the meaning of Penal Code sections 12022.5(a)(1) and 12022.53(b).

* * * * *

Principals

Lana Clarkson: VICTIM, actress (*Fast Times at Ridgemont High, Barbarian Queen*) and door security (VIP Hostess) at the Foundation Room, House of Blues, Sunset Strip. Age 40.

Phillip Spector: DEFENDANT, famous record producer (Ike and Tina Turner, The Ronettes, The Beatles, The Ramones) known for the "Wall of Sound" technique. Inducted into the Rock and Roll Hall of Fame 1989. Age 63.

Others, in Alphabetical Order

Dr. John Andrews: Deputy Medical Examiner, County of Los Angeles, Department of Coroner. Testified for the Prosecution

Linda Kenney-Baden: One of Mr. Spector's lawyers. Married to Dr. Michael Baden

Dr. Michael Baden: Leading forensic expert — testified for the Defense. Married to Linda Kenney-Baden

Michelle Blaine: Mr. Spector's assistant

Lisa Bloom: Correspondent for TruTV

Sara Caplan: One of Mr. Spector's initial lawyers in the criminal case (filed *Caplan v. S.C.L.A. et al.* on June 25, 2007)

Brandon Cardella: Alhambra California Police Department Officer

Donna Clarkson: Lana Clarkson's mother

Bruce Cutler: One of the lawyers in Mr. Spector's third set of lawyers. Either quit or was fired by Mr. Spector before closing arguments in the first trial. Former defense counsel for reputed mob boss John ("Teflon Don") Gotti

Rommie Davis: Female friend of Phil Spector and former high school classmate

Adriano DeSouza: Mr. Spector's chauffeur the evening of the shooting

Vincent DiMaio: Forensic expert on gunshot wounds. Testified for the Defense

Truc Do: Deputy District Attorney, Los Angeles County

Ricardo Enriquez: Juror #9 in first Spector trial — voted guilty

Judge Larry Paul Fidler: Los Angeles Superior Court Judge

Jody "Babydol" Gibson: Owner and operator of a female "escort" service — later convicted of felony pimping — author of *Secrets of a Hollywood Super Madam*

| Ms. Clarkson | Phil Spector, photo taken in jail |

Officer Derek Gilliam: Alhambra California Police Department Officer

James Hammond: Alhambra California Police Department Officer

Dr. Lynne Herold: Los Angeles County Sheriff's Office Senior Criminalist. Testified for the Prosecution

Nili Hudson: Friend of Lana Clarkson

Alan Jackson: Deputy District Attorney, Los Angeles County. Lead prosecution attorney, Phil Spector trial

Detective/Sergeant Katz: Los Angeles Sheriff's Department — Homicide Division

Garrett Kennedy: Alhambra California Police Department Officer

Irene Elizabeth Laughlin (Punkin' Pie): Friend of Lana Clarkson

Dr. Henry Lee: Renowned forensic scientist

Detective Lilienfeld: Los Angeles Sheriff's Department — Homicide Division

Jamie Lintemoot: Criminalist, Los Angeles Coroner's Office

Elizabeth F. Loftus: Distinguished Professor of Social Ecology, and Professor of Law and Cognitive Science, University of California at Irvine. Testified for the Defense

Dr. Robert Alan Middleburg: Toxicologist/criminalist. Testified for the Defense

Corporal Mike Page: Alhambra California Police Department Officer

Dr. Lewis Peña: Los Angeles County Deputy Coroner. Performed autopsy on Ms. Clarkson. Testified for the Prosecution

Corporal/Detective Esther Pineda: Alhambra California Police Department Officer

Steven Renteria: Los Angeles Sheriff's Department Criminalist. Testified for the Prosecution

Jennifer Hayes-Riedl: Friend of Lana Clarkson

Dennis P. Riordan: One of Mr. Spector's attorneys at his first trial; attorney for Mr. Spector on appeal

Bea Rodriguez: Alhambra California Police Department Officer

Charles Sevilla: Attorney for Mr. Spector on appeal

Robert Shapiro: Mr. Spector's original attorney for this case. Formerly represented O.J. Simpson

Gregory Sims: Screenwriter, independent film producer

Nicole Spector: Mr. Spector's daughter

Rachelle (Short) Spector: Mr. Spector's wife — married after shooting occurred

Dr. Werner Spitz: Forensic expert. Testified for the Defense

Kathy Sullivan: A waitress and friend of Mr. Spector

Vincent Tannazzo: Former New York City police detective. Provided security at holiday parties for Joan Rivers

Doron Weinberg: Attorney, Weinberg & Wilder, San Francisco, California. Mr. Spector's attorney for criminal trial number two.

RULES OF EVIDENCE
AND THE SPECTOR TRIAL

The Federal Rules of Evidence control what information and evidence a party is allowed to present at trial. Prior to 1975, there was no uniform set of rules that told lawyers and judges what information could be submitted at trial. Instead, lawyers looked to prior decisions of courts for guidance. Because of this lack of a standard, often times courts in one area of the country would reach decisions different from other areas of the country. The result was that trial outcomes were not uniform. In 1958, the American Bar Association urged the United States Judicial Conference (an administrative body of the Federal courts) to consider adopting uniform rules. It took until July 1, 1975, for these uniform rules to actually be adopted.

The adopted rules purposely keep some evidence from the jury so it never sees or hears it. Why would we want to purposely exclude evidence? For various public policy reasons; to promote certain ideals of America; to make sure the defendant in a criminal case receives a fair trial; to ensure that the trial runs smoothly; to make sure witnesses are protected from embarrassing questions, among other reasons. While the goal is to get to the truth, the rules help make the process more fair.

The rules of evidence are also divided into several different categories. Each category is numbered separately, but sequentially. For example, Relevancy is numbered in the 400s and Privileges is numbered in the 500s. This system makes it much easier to find the rule for which you are looking. The rules are divided into the following general categories:

➤ General Provisions (100s)
➤ Judicial Notice (200s)
➤ Presumptions (300s)
➤ Relevancy and Its Limits (400s)
➤ Privileges (500s)
➤ Witnesses (600s)
➤ Opinions and Expert Testimony (700s)
➤ Hearsay (800s)
➤ Authentication and Identification (900s)
➤ Contents of Writings, Recordings, and Photographs (1000s)
➤ Miscellaneous Rules (1100s)

It is important to remember that while the rules are divided into categories, they are also intertwined. Evidence must comply with all of the rules before it can be admitted. Simply because the evidence would be admissible under one rule does not mean that it will not be excluded because of another. In other words, if a lawyer proves that a particular piece of evidence is relevant, it may still be excluded because it is hearsay. Any particular piece of evidence must be admissible under all of the rules. On the other hand, the opposing counsel has the responsibility to object to the evidence, and must object on all possible grounds.

ARTICLE I. GENERAL PROVISIONS

Rule 101. Scope

These rules govern proceedings in the courts of the United States and before United States bankruptcy judges and United States magistrate judges, to the extent and with the exceptions stated in Rule 1101.

This is an actual case. It is *The People of the State of California v. Phillip Spector*, Case # BA 255233, tried in the Superior Court for the State of California, County of Los Angeles, before the Honorable Judge Larry Paul Fidler. All rulings were made under the California Evidence Code. The California rules are available at: http://law.justia.com/california/codes/evid.html. All analysis of evidence in this book will be considered under the Federal Rules of Evidence, available at: http://www.law.cornell.edu/rules/fre/. For an excellent analysis and comparison of the California Evidence Code and the Federal Rules of Evidence, See Miguel A. Mendez, Evidence — A Concise Comparison of the Federal Rules with the California Code, West, publishers.

Rule 102. Purpose and Construction

These rules shall be construed to secure fairness in administration, elimination of unjustifiable expense and delay, and promotion of growth and development of the law of evidence to the end that the truth may be ascertained and proceedings justly determined.

Rule 103. Rulings on Evidence

(a) Effect of erroneous ruling.
Error may not be predicated upon a ruling which admits or excludes evidence unless a substantial right of the party is affected, and
  (1) Objection. — In case the ruling is one admitting evidence, a timely objection or motion to strike appears of record, stating the specific ground of objection, if the specific ground was not apparent from the context; or
  (2) Offer of proof. — In case the ruling is one excluding evidence, the substance of the evidence was made known to the court by offer or was apparent from the context within which questions were asked.
Once the court makes a definitive ruling on the record admitting or excluding evidence, either at or before trial, a party need not renew an objection or offer of proof to preserve a claim of error for appeal.

(b) Record of offer and ruling.
The court may add any other or further statement which shows the character of the evidence, the form in which it was offered, the objection made, and the ruling thereon. It may direct the making of an offer in question and answer form.

(c) Hearing of jury.

In jury cases, proceedings shall be conducted, to the extent practicable, so as to prevent inadmissible evidence from being suggested to the jury by any means, such as making statements or offers of proof or asking questions in the hearing of the jury.

(d) Plain error.

Nothing in this rule precludes taking notice of plain errors affecting substantial rights although they were not brought to the attention of the court.

There were many *motions in limine* in the *People v. Spector* case. Arguably the most significant of these was the State of California's Motion in Limine to Admit Evidence of Other Crimes filed on February 17, 2005 (refilled for the second trial on August 14, 2008). The State's theory was that Phil Spector had a history of gun violence, particularly against women. The State filed the motion *in limine* to allow this prior "bad act" evidence. The judge granted this motion in part and denied it in part. The defense also filed many motions *in limine*; one was to prevent the prosecution from introducing pictures of the jacket worn by Mr. Spector on the evening in question. The jacket had colored arrows (applied by the State) pointing to alleged blood stains. The defense further moved to exclude any evidence of Mr. Spector's blood alcohol level that was tested the day after the death of Lana Clarkson, while Mr. Spector was in custody at the Alhambra jail.

Judge Fidler also made some rulings on jury instructions that led to objections by the defense. He allowed a jury instruction in the second trial that the jury could consider involuntary manslaughter in addition to the second-degree murder charge. He denied a State request for this instruction in the first trial.

In addition, during the first trial jury deliberation, Judge Fidler withdrew an instruction and substituted a new one, leading to a strong objection from the defense. The defense argued that the substitution was inappropriate because the jury had indicated to the judge that it was at an impasse. The foreman had indicated to the judge that the jury was at a 7-5 split, although the judge did not inquire about which way the jury was leaning — toward conviction or innocence. The original instruction was that the jury had to find that Mr. Spector held the gun that went off in Ms. Clarkson's mouth. The substituted instruction was the following:

In order to convict Mr. Spector, you must find that he "committed an act with a firearm that caused the death of Lana Clarkson, such as:

a. Placing the gun in her mouth or forcing her to place the gun in her mouth at which time it discharged;

b. Pointing the gun at or against her head, at which time it entered her mouth and discharged;

c. Pointing the gun at her to prevent her from leaving his house, causing a struggle which resulted in the gun entering her mouth and discharging."

Doron Weinberg, Mr. Spector's counsel, indicated that he planned to appeal the conviction on the grounds that the judge erred when he allowed five women to testify about prior instances of gun violence. Indeed, Mr. Spector has appealed his conviction on this ground (among others), although Mr. Weinberg no longer represents Mr. Spector. Some legal commentators also believe the changes in jury instructions were grounds for appeal, had the jury convicted Mr. Spector in the first trial.

Judge Fidler also issued gag orders against individuals, most notably Rachelle Spector, Mr. Spector's wife, and Jody Gibson, a potential witness. During the trial the Los Angeles Sheriff's Department investigated a "MySpace" entry that was considered a threat to the judge. The following is the text of the entry:

I love Phil Spector — — !!!!
The Evil Judge Should Die!!!!
Xoxo Chelle

The Sheriff's Office investigated whether the entry was made by Rachelle Spector. Mr. Spector's attorneys denied that Rachelle was the author of the entry. No finding of authorship was ever made.

The Defense filed a motion under California Code of Civil Procedure to disqualify Judge Fidler from presiding over the second trial of Mr. Spector. This motion was denied on March 18, 2008 and Judge Fidler did in fact preside over Mr. Spector's second trial.

Questions

103-1 Was a "substantial right" of Mr. Spector "affected" by Judge Fidler's ruling that prior "bad act" evidence was admissible? Was this plain error so that a new trial would be ordered even in the absence of an objection?

103-2 Was a "substantial right" of Mr. Spector "affected" by Judge Fidler's ruling that Mr. Spector's jacket with the arrows showing blood and his blood alcohol level was admissible?

103-3 Were Judge Fidler's rulings on jury instructions in the first trial correct? If incorrect, would a new trial have been appropriate?

103-4 May a judge preside over the second trial of a defendant? May a judge issue "gag orders" to non-witnesses?

Rule 104. Preliminary Questions

(a) Questions of admissibility generally.

Preliminary questions concerning the qualification of a person to be a witness, the existence of a privilege, or the admissibility of evidence shall be determined by the court, subject to the provisions of subdivision (b). In making its determination it is not bound by the rules of evidence except those with respect to privileges.

(b) Relevancy conditioned on fact.

When the relevancy of evidence depends upon the fulfillment of a condition of fact, the court shall admit it upon, or subject to, the introduction of evidence sufficient to support a finding of the fulfillment of the condition.

(c) Hearing of jury.

Hearings on the admissibility of confessions shall in all cases be conducted out of the hearing of the jury. Hearings on other preliminary matters shall be so conducted when the interests of justice require, or when an accused is a witness and so requests.

(d) Testimony by accused.

The accused does not, by testifying upon a preliminary matter, become subject to cross-examination as to other issues in the case.

(e) Weight and credibility.

This rule does not limit the right of a party to introduce before the jury evidence relevant to weight or credibility.

Rule 105. Limited Admissibility

When evidence which is admissible as to one party or for one purpose but not admissible as to another party or for another purpose is admitted, the court, upon request, shall restrict the evidence to its proper scope and instruct the jury accordingly.

ARTICLE II. JUDICIAL NOTICE

Rule 201. Judicial Notice of Adjudicative Facts

(a) Scope of rule.

This rule governs only judicial notice of adjudicative facts.

(b) Kinds of facts.

A judicially noticed fact must be one not subject to reasonable dispute in that it is either (1) generally known within the territorial jurisdiction of the trial court or (2) capable of accurate and ready determination by resort to sources whose accuracy cannot reasonably be questioned.

(c) When discretionary.

A court may take judicial notice, whether requested or not.

(d) When mandatory.

A court shall take judicial notice if requested by a party and supplied with the necessary information.

(e) Opportunity to be heard.

A party is entitled upon timely request to an opportunity to be heard as to the propriety of taking judicial notice and the tenor of the matter noticed. In the absence of prior notification, the request may be made after judicial notice has been taken.

(f) Time of taking notice.

Judicial notice may be taken at any stage of the proceeding.

(g) Instructing jury.

In a civil action or proceeding, the court shall instruct the jury to accept as conclusive any fact judicially noticed. In a criminal case, the court shall instruct the jury that it may, but is not required to, accept as conclusive any fact judicially noticed.

ARTICLE III. PRESUMPTIONS IN CIVIL ACTIONS AND PROCEEDINGS

Rule 301. Presumptions in General Civil Actions and Proceedings

In all civil actions and proceedings not otherwise provided for by Act of Congress or by these rules, a presumption imposes on the party against whom it is directed the burden of going forward with evidence to rebut or meet the presumption, but does not shift to such party the burden of proof in the sense of the risk of nonpersuasion, which remains throughout the trial upon the party on whom it was originally cast.

Questions

301-1   In the civil case *Donna Clarkson v. Phil Spector*, which party has the burden of proof?

301-2   In the civil case *Donna Clarkson v. Phil Spector*, which party has the burden of production?

ARTICLE IV. RELEVANCY AND ITS LIMITS

Rule 401. Definition of "Relevant Evidence"

"Relevant evidence" means evidence having any tendency to make the existence of any fact that is of consequence to the determination of the action more probable or less probable than it would be without the evidence.

What is a "fact of consequence"? An item of evidence has no relevance in a vacuum. There must be some relationship between the piece of evidence and the fact sought to be proved. A gun, in and of itself, has no relevance. However, it begins to have some relevance if the crime in issue has been committed with a gun — an armed robbery, for example. Yet this fact may not be "consequential" enough. There must be a tie between the particular gun in issue and the crime. What type of gun fired the bullets? If a witness saw the weapon, was it a shotgun or a revolver? In the Phil Spector trial, the shot that killed Lana was a bullet from a .38 caliber Colt blue steel revolver. At issue was not the revolver itself, but who actually fired the shot — was it Lana (a suicide), or Phil (a murder)? A "fact of consequence" is one that makes a difference. The fact to be proved is relevant if "it is of consequence in the determination of the action," according to the Advisory Committee to the Federal Rules of Evidence. "Relevancy is not an inherent characteristic of any item of evidence but exists only as a relation between an item of evidence and a matter properly provable in the case. Does the item of evidence tend to prove the matter sought to be proved?" For example, a gun is brought into court. In order to be relevant, it must be shown that the gun was actually the gun found at the scene of the crime — the one missing the bullet — the one found under her leg. If the parties agree that a particular gun was involved in the altercation, is the make and model of the gun important? Is it something about which we care?

"More probable or less probable" — what exactly does this mean? This is generally referred to as "probative value." Does the piece of evidence (e.g., gun, bloody knife) have any tendency to make the existence of a fact (e.g., the victim was stabbed) to the issue sought to be proved (e.g., defendant stabbed the victim) any more likely or less likely? Does the evidence have probative value? Does it tend to prove or disprove something?

Of course, it is impossible to determine whether something is relevant without considering the issues in the case. If it is a civil case, as is *Donna Clarkson v. Phil Spector*, it is necessary to look at the pleadings — the complaint and the answer, as well as any subsequent filings. In a criminal case, as in *State of California v. Phillip Spector*, it is necessary to consider the elements of the crimes alleged as well as any asserted defenses.

Is the fact that Lana Clarkson went shopping for shoes with her mother Donna Clarkson the day before she died *relevant*?

In the civil case, Donna Clarkson asserts wrongful death, negligence, and battery. Donna Clarkson alleges that Phil Spector shot and killed her daughter and "grabbed, hit, fought with, restrained and otherwise prevented the departure from his home, and injured decedent Lana Clarkson." Certainly the shoe shopping seems to have no connection with the civil case. In the wrongful death pleading, it is alleged that Phil Spector's wrongful conduct caused Lana's death and as a proximate result, Donna Clarkson "sustained pecuniary loss resulting from the loss of society, love, care, comfort, support, attention, protection, services, and financial support, as well as other benefits and assistance of the decedent." Is the shoe shopping trip now relevant?

Phil Spector's defense in the criminal case is that Lana Clarkson committed suicide. During his opening statement, Spector attorney Doron Weinberg stated that Lana Clarkson had recently turned 40 and had experienced personal and career setbacks. She was depressed and suicidal and took her own life at Mr. Spector's residence it was alleged. Is the allegation that Phil and Rachelle Spector failed to pay over $104,000 to the Bonaventure Hotel & Suites in Los Angeles during the pendency of the first criminal trial *relevant*?

Assume the allegation about the hotel is true. Does it make it any more likely or less likely that Mr. Spector murdered Ms. Clarkson? Does it make it any more likely or less likely that he grabbed, hit, or fought with Ms. Clarkson? No. It has no probative value.

On May 14, 2004, there was a report of an altercation at Mr. Spector's residence (the castle). When the police arrived, the police learned that an argument between Mr. Spector and his driver Tobey Wheeler had turned physical. Both men requested that the other man be arrested for assault and battery. The two men were taken to the police station. The police later declined to prosecute.

Questions

401-1 Is the make or model of the gun in the *Spector* case a fact of consequence?

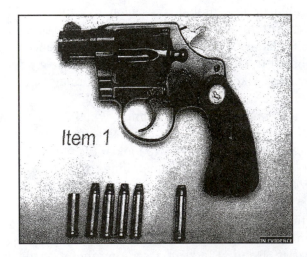

401-2 Is the fact that Lana went shoe shopping a fact of consequence in either the civil or criminal trial? In what way does it make the murder or suicide allegation more likely or less likely?

401-3   Is the altercation at Mr. Spector's residence on May 14, 2004, relevant to the Phil Spector murder case?

401-4   Is "any tendency" a strict standard? What if a piece of evidence has only a slight amount of probative value?

Rule 402. Relevant Evidence Generally Admissible; Irrelevant Evidence Inadmissible

All relevant evidence is admissible, except as otherwise provided by the Constitution of the United States, by Act of Congress, by these rules, or by other rules prescribed by the Supreme Court pursuant to statutory authority. Evidence which is not relevant is not admissible.

Relevant evidence is admissible (provided it falls within the other Rules of Evidence) and irrelevant evidence is not admissible. Seems rather obvious, does it not?

In what circumstances would evidence that is relevant be prohibited as evidence due to the U.S. Constitution or an Act of Congress? One category is evidence that violates the Fourth Amendment right of an individual to be free from unreasonable searches and seizures. In this case, there was no argument made that the police had violated the Fourth Amendment. They were called to the scene of a shooting and were entitled to secure the residence.

After they had handcuffed Mr. Spector, the police officers went up the stairs to the second floor of the mansion. There they saw many items that would later be entered into evidence. At approximately 4 P.M. on February 3, 2003, the police executed search warrants and actually recovered the evidence.

One of the key pieces of evidence was a wet and bloody diaper found in the upstairs bathroom. The prosecution contended at trial that Mr. Spector wiped his bloody hands on the diaper. Some may wonder why a diaper was located at Mr. Spector's residence. One speculation is that it could have been there because sometimes diapers are used as cleaning cloths.

Questions

402-1   Is the bloody diaper relevant?

402-2   If the bloody diaper was obtained through an illegal search and seizure would Rule 402 come into play?

Rule 403. Exclusion of Relevant Evidence on Grounds of Prejudice, Confusion, or Waste of Time

Although relevant, evidence may be excluded if its probative value is substantially outweighed by the danger of unfair prejudice, confusion of the issues, or misleading the jury, or by considerations of undue delay, waste of time, or needless presentation of cumulative evidence.

State of California
County of Los Angeles

Page 1 of 4

Receipt for Property Taken on Search Warrant

Following is a detailed list of property taken by me under
the authority of a search warrant issued the 3rd day of
FEB '03, 19___ , in the Los Angeles County SUPERIOR Court,
Department/Division, ELA .

1) COLT 2", B/S REV. 38 CA, # B
2) BRN LTHL HOLSTER W/ BLOOD
3) TASER MATERIAL
4) BRASS FROM DEAD BOLT ON BK DOOR
5) POSS. FINGERNAIL, TEETH & WOOD CHIP MATTER
6) TASER MATERIAL
7) STATUE
8) BRN VALISE W/ MISC I.D., PHONES, WLT, CAMERA
   GLASSES, PAPERS, CD PLAYER
9) BLOOD FROM RAIL
10) POSS TOOTH (ON STAIRS)
11) POSS NAIL (ON STAIRS)
12) FACE TOWEL FROM BATH ROOM
13) FALSE EYE LASHES FROM BATHROOM
14) BLOODY RAG FROM BATHROOM FLOOR
15) CANADA DRY BOTTLE

An undetermined amount of U.S. Currency was seized as a
result of the above warrant. An audit of the amount seized
was impractical under the present conditions. An accurate
count of the funds seized will be made and a receipt will be
delivered to this location within five business days.

SIGNED MARK LILLIENFELD   EMPLOYEE #

LOS ANGELES COUNTY SHERIFF'S DEPARTMENT

2/3/03   1955

ATTY. ROGER SHANN

REPORT CONTINUATION ... NARRATIVE	URN

16) JOSE CUERVO BOTTLE

17) BRANDY GLASS (LVG ROOM)

18) LIGHTER (LVG RM)

19) WHT COAT (FLOOR OF UPSTAIRS DRESSING RM)

20) BLOOD ON DOOR STRIKER PLATE

21) ALLEGRA RX PKG IN TRASH (BATHROOM)

22) BLU COMB (BATHRM SINK)

23) HAIR SPRAY CAN (BATHRM SINK)

24) BRANDY GLASS (SINK)

25) .357, S&W, REV, W/ 6 .38 RDS, # K

26) .38, S&W, REV, W/ 5 .38 RDS, # J

27) .9 MM BROWNING PISTOL, UNK #

28) 6 LIVE 9 MM RDS, W/W, AMMO

29) MISC .38 & 9 MM ROUNDS OF AMMO

30) 1 BOX OF 38 CA. RDS

31) .25 CA PISTOL, STAR, W/ HOLSTER, #8

32) SAFARLAND HOLSTER

33) CROSSMAN AIR GUN

34) SHOTGUN (NOT SIEZED-PHOTOGRAPHED ONLY)

35) BLK BASKET WEAVE HOLSTER

36) (2) LATEX GLOVES

37) MISC BEDDING FROM MASTER BD RM.

38) LATEX GLOVE (UPSTAIRS BAR)

39) SANITARY NAPKIN (WEST, GRND FLOOR BATHROOM
    NXT TO KITCHEN)

40) WHT WOOD CHAIR W/ CUSHION (FOYER, VICT WAS
    FOUND DECEASED IN)

41) 2" B/S STAINER PISTOL IN ___ 2/3/05 14885
    HOLSTER.

76R288M—Sn-R-313— PS 10-82

REPORT CONTINUATION — NARRATIVE	URN

42) SANITARY NAPKIN, (FROM TRASH CAN IN 2ND STORY BATHRM - S. OF OFFICE, W. OF KITCHEN)

42) LETTER, DATE 10-10-2000, TO NANCY

✱ ITEMS SIEZED BY DET. LINDA MUSE, C̄ ACCOUNTED FOR AFTER ATTY SHAPIRO SIGNED ORIG. RECEIPT.

SONY, HANDY CAM CORDER, S/N # 254665

PANASONIC, DIGITAL, 300 X, PALM, RECORDER, S/N # PVL750D

FOUR 8 MM TAPES

✱ ITEM SIEZED BY DET. ROBERT KENNEY N ACCOUNTED FOR AFTER ATTY SHAPIRO SIGNED ORIG. RECEIPT.

SEXUAL ASSAULT KIT ON PHILLIP SPECTOR.

2/3/03 1955

76R288M—Sh-R-313— PS 10-82

LOS ANGELES COUNTY SHERIFF'S DEPARTMENT - DETECTIVE DIVISION

SEARCH ~~WARRANT~~ ~~INVENTORY~~

DATE: 2-4-03   TIME: 1615 HRS.

LOCATION: 1700 S. GRANDVIEW , ALHAMBRA

SEARCHER(S): KERFOOT / BIEHN

FILE #: 003- 00017- 3199- 011

****

ITEM DESCRIPTION   *ALL ITEMS RECOVERED FROM 2ND FLOOR OF   LOCATION FOUND

1- COLT, .38 CAL, ARMY SPECIAL, REV, SN 46

1- COLT, .38 CAL, DET. SPECIAL, REV, SN 3

1- S&W, .357 CAL, MODEL 27-2, REV, SN N

1- S&W, .38 CAL, MODEL 60, REV, SN R

1- HIGH STANDARD, .22 CAL, SENTINEL, REV, SN 1

5- BROWN LEATHER HOLSTERS

1- BOX LABELED "SPEER" AMMO, CONT. 24 LIVE SPEER ROUNDS,
    4 LIVE R-P ROUNDS, 1 LIVE FEDERAL ROUND - ALL .38 CAL.

1- PLASTIC CONTAINER OF AMMO CONT. MISC CALIBERS OF AMMUNITION.

1- COTTON CLOTH APPROX 8"X14"

1- COLT, .38 CAL, DET. SPECIAL, REV, SN A 43406

1- BLACK GUN CASE FOR ABOVE GUN

1- LAP TOP COMPUTER W/ CASE & MOUSE "APPLE" BRAND, SN UV23118HLQ0

1- COMPUTER, APPLE I-MAC, W/ KEYBOARD & MOUSE SN QT212H1BL3V

1- ZIP DRIVE, SN PSAW50EO1P

4- ZIP DISKS

1- 3½" FLOPPY DISK

1- PRINTER, EPSON, MODEL P 340A, SN D33E438893

BIEHN #096551 2/3/03 1955
Biehn L.A.S.D.
HOMICIDE

31

The standard for relevance from Rule 401 is quite relaxed. The "any tendency" language sets the bar low. Once something is deemed relevant under Rule 401, are there some reasons for excluding the evidence nevertheless? Yes. Rule 403 is used extensively to exclude otherwise relevant evidence. This rule allows the exclusion of evidence if the evidence is misleading, cumulative, or would lead to a waste of time, undue delay, or confusion. The main use of Rule 403, however, is to exclude unduly prejudicial, but relevant, evidence. Notice that the exclusion is proper when the probative value is *substantially outweighed* by the prejudicial effect. Presumably every piece of evidence is prejudicial. It should be or one questions why it would ever be offered into evidence by a party. It is only when there is a complete imbalance that the evidence should be excluded. It is a question of fact for the judge. Consider the following proposed pieces of evidence:

1. Defense proposed evidence that Lana Clarkson knew how to handle a gun — as shown by DVD clips of her acting in T.V. and movies.
2. Defense proposed evidence of Lana Clarkson's computer "memoir" where she wrote about cocaine use in her youth.
3. Defense proposed evidence of testimony and documents of Jody "Babydol" Gibson. Gibson was convicted of three counts of solicitation and pimping

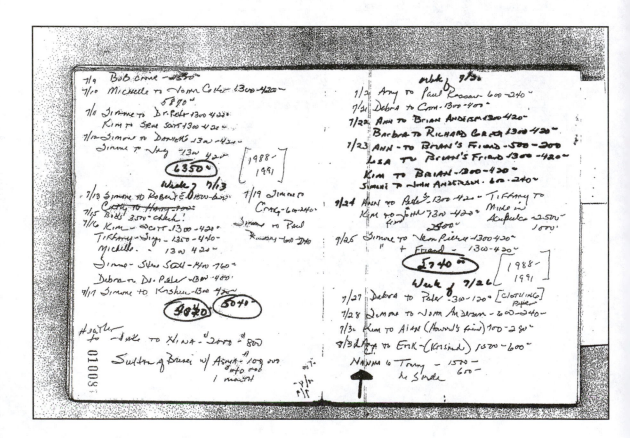

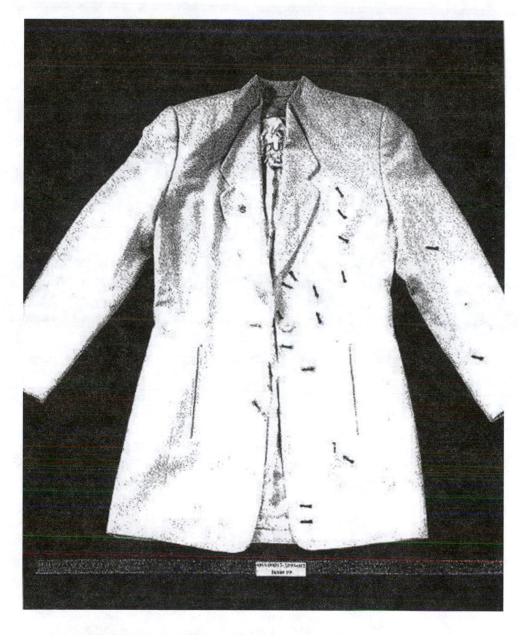

in 2000 in case #LA033582. She served her three-year sentence and was out of prison. The defense proposed both her testimony and an entry in her "black book" to allegedly prove that Lana Clarkson had been one of her prostitutes (see entry 8/3 "Lana to Eric"). The prosecution asserted that the entry in the black book was altered.

4. Defense *Motion in Limine* to "Prevent the Prosecution from Either Displaying Pictures of the Jacket Worn by Mr. Spector Which Contain Colored Arrows or Displaying the Jacket Itself with Colored Arrows on It."

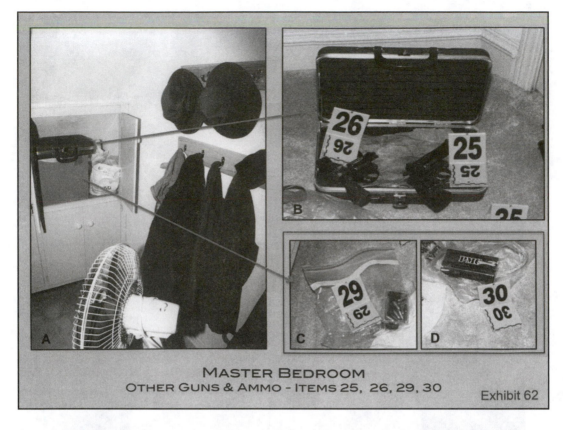

MASTER BEDROOM
OTHER GUNS & AMMO - ITEMS 25, 26, 29, 30

Exhibit 62

5. Defense *Motion in Limine* to "Exclude Prosecution Evidence of Phillip Spector's Estimated Blood Alcohol Level at Time of Shooting." The prosecution planned to extrapolate Mr. Spector's blood alcohol level at the time of the shooting by introducing evidence of his blood alcohol tests administered 12 hours later. The State also planned to introduce expert testimony of the average blood alcohol level given a certain number of drinks.

6. The defense filed a *Motion in Limine* to exclude evidence that the police recovered 11 firearms at Mr. Spector's residence the date of his arrest.

Questions

403-1 Is each of the above pieces of evidence relevant under Rule 401?

403-2 Should each of the above pieces of evidence be excluded by Rule 403 because its probative value is substantially outweighed by its prejudicial effect?

403-3 How should the Court rule on the discovery of 11 firearms at Mr. Spector's residence?

403-4 The defense wishes to show a photograph of Ms. Clarkson's "excised tongue, marked with cuts and bruises" into evidence. How should the Court rule?

403-5   The State wishes to show a photograph of Ms. Clarkson as she was found on the morning of the shooting. Is this photo too graphic? Would it inflame the emotions of the jurors?

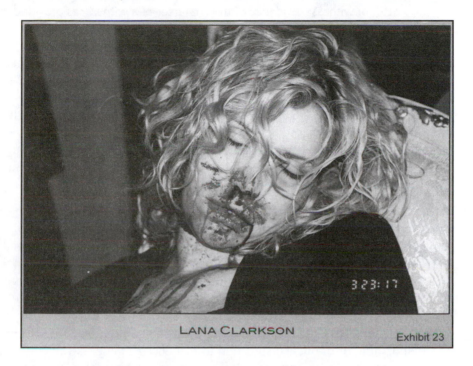

LANA CLARKSON

3 23: 17

Exhibit 23

403-6   Officer Tannazzo testified at Mr. Spector's trial that at Joan Rivers's Christmas party, Mr. Spector said to him, "that's why I have these permits. I carry a piece, these f***ing *unts . . . they all deserve a bullet in their f***ing heads." Are these statements too prejudicial? Could part of the statement be admissible and other parts inadmissable?

Rule 404. Character Evidence Not Admissible to Prove Conduct; Exceptions; Other Crimes

(a) Character evidence generally

Evidence of a person's character or a trait of character is not admissible for the purpose of proving action in conformity therewith on a particular occasion, except:

(1) Character of accused — In a criminal case, evidence of a pertinent trait of character offered by an accused, or by the prosecution to rebut the same, or if evidence of a trait of character of the alleged victim of the crime is offered by an accused and admitted under Rule 404(a)(2), evidence of the same trait of character of the accused offered by the prosecution;

(2) Character of alleged victim — In a criminal case, and subject to the limitations imposed by Rule 412, evidence of a pertinent trait of character of the alleged victim of the crime offered by an accused, or by the prosecution to rebut the

same, or evidence of a character trait of peacefulness of the alleged victim offered by the prosecution in a homicide case to rebut evidence that the alleged victim was the first aggressor;

(3) Character of witness — Evidence of the character of a witness, as provided in Rules 607, 608, and 609.

(b) Other crimes, wrongs, or acts

Evidence of other crimes, wrongs, or acts is not admissible to prove the character of a person in order to show action in conformity therewith. It may, however, be admissible for other purposes, such as proof of motive, opportunity, intent, preparation, plan, knowledge, identity, or absence of mistake or accident, provided that upon request by the accused, the prosecution in a criminal case shall provide reasonable notice in advance of trial, or during trial if the court excuses pretrial notice on good cause shown, of the general nature of any such evidence it intends to introduce at trial.

The first part of this Rule, 404(a), is the general rule prohibiting the use of character evidence. The second part, Rule 404(b), is generally referred to as "other bad act" evidence. The general rule is that character evidence is not allowed. There are exceptions to this general prohibition of this use of character at trial. Character evidence played a large role in the *Spector* trial. One of the main arguments in Mr. Spector's appeal is the improper admission of character evidence.

First, what exactly is "character?" According to the Advisory Committee Notes to the Federal Rules (Rule 406), "Character is a generalized description of one's disposition, or of one's disposition in respect to a general trait, such as honesty, temperance, or peacefulness." A tendency toward violence has been found to be a character trait.

The rules on Character are easier to understand if one looks first to the question — Whose character is being offered in evidence? The Rules are divided along the following lines:

1. Character of the Defendant — Rule 404(a)(1) and (b)
2. Character of the Victim — Rule 404(a)(2)
3. Character of a Witness — Rules 608 and 609

Technically, Rule 404(b) is for "person" so, presumably, it could apply to a defendant, a victim, or a witness. It also applies in both criminal and civil cases. With respect to witnesses, courts would generally look to the more specific rule on witnesses, Rules 608 and 609. However, as a practical matter it most often applies to a defendant in a criminal case. This rule is a general prohibition against what is called "propensity evidence." According to the Merriam-Webster dictionary, propensity means "an . . . intense natural inclination or preference." Under the U.S. system of justice, we have rejected the use of evidence of bad character to show that a person acted in a particular manner on a particular occasion. "Character evidence . . . tends to distract the trier of fact from the main question of what actually happened on the particular occasion. It subtly permits the trier of fact to reward the good man and to punish the bad man because of their respective characters despite what the evidence in the case shows actually happened." Advisory Committee Comments to Federal Rule of Evidence 404, citing to the California Law Revision Commission. Our Federal Rules follow the Common Law tradition "to disallow resort by the prosecution to any kind of evidence of a defendant's evil character to establish a probability of his guilt." *Old Chief v. United States*, 519 U.S. 172, 181 (1997). The Advisory Committee believed character evidence had limited relevance. However, others have commented that character evidence has too much relevance. It has too much probative value and the risk is that the jury will find a defendant guilty of the crime in issue because he or she is a bad person. The "she did it before, she did it this time" mentality. The character evidence "tends to distract the trier of fact from the main question of what actually happened on a particular occasion." *Jones v. Southern Pacific Railroad*, 962 F.2d 447, 449 (5th Cir. 1992). "The jury's determination of guilt or innocence should be based on evidence relevant to the crime charged." *United States v. Turquitt*, 557 F.2d 464, 468 (5th Cir. 1977). As with any good rule, there are of course exceptions.

Character of the Defendant   Since 2006, Rule 404(a)(1) applies only to criminal defendants. Prior to that, it was unclear if it applied in both civil and criminal cases. It has been the rule for many years that an accused may introduce his or her character into evidence. This is referred to as the "mercy rule." The belief is that the defendant's life or liberty is at issue in a criminal case and therefore he or she should be able to offer his or her own character into evidence. Presumably, this would be good character — for example, the character of an accused for peacefulness or honesty. The defendant is permitted to use character as "good" propensity evidence, for example, that he or she is known as a peaceful person and thus acted in a peaceful manner on the particular occasion in issue. The general rule against propensity evidence is not applied when used by the accused. *United States v. Yarbrough*, 527 F.3d 1092 (10th Cir. 2008).

"The rule prohibiting circumstantial use of character evidence 'was relaxed to allow the criminal defendant with so much at stake and so little available in the way of conventional proof to have special dispensation to tell the factfinder just what sort of person he really is.'" Richard Uviller, *Evidence of Character to Prove Conduct: Illusion, Illogic, and Injustice in the Courtroom*, 130 U. Pa .L. Rev. 845, 855 (1982), as cited in the Advisory Committee Notes to the 2006 Amendment to Rule 404.

There is a potential high cost to this use of good character, however. If the defendant offers his or her good character in evidence, the prosecution may counter with evidence of bad character (the defendant has "opened the door" to this bad character evidence). *Michelson v. United States*, 335 U.S. 469, 479 (1948) and *United States v. Moore*, 27 F.3d 969, 974 (4th Cir. 1994). In other words, the prosecution in a criminal case is prohibited from presenting "bad" character evidence of a defendant to a judge or a jury, except in very limited circumstances (Rule 404(b)). However, if the defendant "opens the door" by presenting his or her own good character, the prosecution may counter with evidence of the defendant's bad character. The door is only open to the same character trait as that offered by the defendant. If the defendant presents evidence of his or her peacefulness, then the prosecution may only offer evidence of his or her past violent tendencies. The prosecution may not offer evidence of his or her truthfulness.

The defendant may testify *directly* about his or her own good character, or he or she may bring in "character witnesses" to testify about either their *opinions* about the defendant's character, or the defendant's general good character *reputation* in the community. A famous case featuring the use of character witnesses is the perjury trial of Alger Hiss in 1950. Hiss was one of the individuals who helped establish the United Nations and was President of the Carnegie Endowment for International Peace. He was accused of being a communist spy during the "Red Scare" and "McCarthyism" of the late 1940s to the late 1950s. Hiss called future Democratic Presidential Candidate Adlai Stevenson, Supreme Court Justice Felix Frankfurter, and former Democratic Presidential Candidate John W. Davis as his character witnesses. Unfortunately for Hiss, the testimonies apparently did little good as he was convicted and served almost four years in prison.

Questions

404-1 May the defense call Phil Spector's daughter Nicole to testify that Mr. Spector was an attentive father?

404-2 May the defense call waitress and friend Kathy Sullivan to testify that Mr. Spector was fatherly? If allowed to testify to this character trait, may the prosecution ask her whether she ever saw him with a gun?

404-3 If Nicole Spector and Kathy Sullivan are allowed to testify as mentioned above, may the prosecution offer evidence of Mr. Spector's alleged violent tendencies?

Character of the Victim Rule 404(a)(2) allows the defendant to present the character of the victim at trial if it is pertinent. This presentation is also allowed under the "mercy rule" theory that the defendant's liberty, and perhaps his or her life, is at stake. The prosecution may not introduce good character of the victim in its case in chief because it is not relevant. It may also be highly prejudicial to the defendant. There is one exception to this rule — in a homicide case the prosecution may introduce the victim's character for peacefulness in its case in chief if the defendant is claiming the victim was the first aggressor.

Generally, the only pertinent trait of character of a victim is the victim's propensity toward violence. The defendant may introduce evidence that he or she acted in self-defense due to the violent character of the victim. In most jurisdictions, the defendant need not have been aware of the victim's violent tendencies at the time of the offense. See *United States v. Keiser*, 57 F.3d 847, 854 (9th Cir. 1995), and *Commonwealth v. Adjutant*, 443 Mass. 649, 824 N.E.2d 1 (2005), footnote 7.

A "double door opening" presents itself if the defense offers into evidence the victim's character. The prosecution may not only introduce rebuttal evidence about the victim, it may also introduce character evidence about the defendant on that same character trait. See 2000 Advisory Committee Notes to Rule 404. Therefore, if the defendant introduces the propensity for violence evidence of the victim, the prosecution may introduce evidence that the victim was peaceful, *and* evidence that the defendant has a character trait of violence.

In the *Spector* case, the defense offered into evidence opinion evidence that Ms. Clarkson was suicidal. Is suicidal a character trait? The defense also attempted to introduce evidence that Ms. Clarkson had a history of illegal drug use.

Questions

404-4   Is evidence that Ms. Clarkson was suicidal admissible under this rule?

404-5   Should the defense be allowed to introduce into evidence Ms. Clarkson's alleged history of illegal drug use?

404-6   May the defense be allowed to bring into evidence Ms. Clarkson's alleged herpes medical condition?

Character of a Witness   Rules for the use of character of a witness at trial are contained in Rules 607 (Who May Impeach), 608 (Evidence of Character and Conduct of a Witness), and 609 (Impeachment by Evidence of Conviction of a Crime).

Other Crimes, Wrongs or Acts   The use of character to show "action in conformity therewith" is strictly prohibited under the Rules, except as provided above. On the other hand, if used to show something else, the use of character is allowed. As examples, and not by way of limitation at all, the Rule lists the allowable use of character to prove motive, opportunity, intent, preparation, plan, knowledge, identity, or absence of mistake or accident. For example, the fact that someone did not report all of his or her income on his or her tax return and was audited by the IRS for several years would not be allowed to show that he or she failed to report the correct amount of tax for the year in issue. It may be allowed, however to show that someone had a *motive* for assaulting an IRS Revenue Agent. In order to show preparation, the government would likely be allowed to introduce evidence that the defendant stole a firearm when later the defendant is tried for premeditated murder.

The "prior bad act" need not be a charged offense. Nor does the defendant need to be arrested or otherwise formally accused of an act. Of course we as a society do not want a prosecutor to be allowed to bring in "other bad act" evidence based only upon a rumor or innuendo. In *Huddleston v. United States*, 485 U.S. 681, 689 (1988), the Supreme Court determined that the level of proof necessary for "other bad act" evidence to be allowed in evidence is "only if the jury can reasonably conclude that the act occurred and that the defendant was the actor." The Court rejected a higher "preponderance of the evidence" standard and found that the level of proof question was answered by Rule 104(b), by simply the fulfillment of a condition.

Prior bad act evidence is allowed in both civil and criminal cases although it most frequently occurs in criminal cases. The overriding prohibitive rule of 403 still applies. *Huddleston*. If the probative value of the prior bad act evidence is substantially outweighed by the prejudicial effect, it is inadmissible. "Evidence is unfairly prejudicial only if it will induce the jury to decide the case on an improper basis, commonly an emotional one rather than on the evidence presented." *United States v. Hicks*, 368 F.3d 801, 807 (7th Cir. 2004).

The prior bad act evidence was the most contested issue in the *Spector* trial. The government planned to introduce a host of prior bad acts into evidence. Some were ruled inadmissible prior to trial, while others were allowed in evidence. One of the main issues on appeal is the admissibility of prior incidents of gun violence.

On February 17, 2005, more than two years before the actual trial, the State of California filed a "Motion in Limine to Admit Evidence of Other Crimes." Specifically, the prosecution sought a ruling on the following prior bad acts (events as alleged by the prosecution):

1. *The 1972 Possession a Loaded Handgun*
   In January 1972, the Beverly Hills Police Department received an anonymous call from a female who indicated that a man in a maroon jacket containing a karate emblem had pointed a gun at her inside the "Daisy Club" on Rodeo Drive. According to the police report the man had become enraged when the female had attempted to engage him in conversation. The man had not invited the woman to engage him in conversation, and in response he drew a gun and pointed it at her. The man was Phil Spector. Officers noticed a bulge underneath Spector's shirt. The officers searched Spector, found a loaded handgun in his waistband, and arrested him. He was charged with a misdemeanor, pleaded guilty, and received one year of probation.

2. *The 1975 Assault at the Beverly Hills Hotel*
   In the early morning hours of November 26, 1975, Kevin Brown, a valet employed by the Beverly Hills Hotel was at work when he heard a woman scream "Get away from me." Brown looked over and saw a man later identified as Mr. Spector arguing with a woman near the front door of the hotel. Brown approached and asked what was happening. Spector turned to face Brown, pointed a revolver at his face, and told Brown, "Get the f*** away from me." Brown began to back away from Spector as Chris Dunn, another valet, approached the group. Spector pointed the gun at Dunn before Spector and another man got into a silver Cadillac and drove away.

   Brown reported the incident to the Beverly Hills Police Department. The Los Angeles County District Attorney charged Spector with two felony counts of assault with a firearm and two misdemeanor counts of brandishing a firearm. In Superior Court, Spector pleaded guilty to one count of misdemeanor brandishing of a firearm. The court placed him on two years of formal probation. A condition of his probation was that he not use or possess any dangerous or deadly weapons.

3. *The 1977 Brandishing of Firearm on Leonard Cohen*
   In 1977, Mr. Spector produced musician Leonard Cohen's record album, *Death of a Ladies Man*. During production of the record, Cohen and Spector, who were friends, were taking a break in the lobby of the music studio. Spector walked up to Cohen, placed one arm around Cohen's shoulders, and pointed a semi-automatic pistol at Cohen's chest with his other hand. Spector told Cohen, "I love you Leonard." Cohen looked at Spector and said, "I hope so, Phil." Spector then walked away from Cohen. No charges were ever filed for this incident.

4. *The 1978 Brandishing of a Firearm on Alan Sacks and Cathy Henderson*
   In 1978, television producer Alan Sacks and his assistant Cathy Henderson arranged to meet with Spector at Spector's Hollywood Hills home in order to discuss the music for a television pilot planned by Sacks. Sacks and Henderson arrived on time and were let into Spector's house by Spector's bodyguard. After letting them in, the bodyguard locked a metal security gate behind them.

   After approximately an hour, Spector came downstairs and asked Sacks what he was doing in his house. Sacks reminded Spector about their appointment. Spector then asked if Sacks had touched anything on the coffee table. When Sacks responded "no," Spector responded, "good, because there would have been a problem." Spector then told Sacks, "you're here because you want to go back and say I drink and like to play with guns." Spector took off his jacket and Sacks could see that Spector was wearing a shoulder holster which contained a handgun.

   Spector pulled the gun in and out of the holster several times and pointed it at Sacks. Sacks had to push the muzzle of the weapon away from him two or three times. Sacks told Spector he wanted to leave. Spector told him not to worry, that he would get out, but did nothing to let him and Henderson out of the house. Spector then led Sacks and Henderson into another room with a piano. Spector began playing songs on the piano, and again took the gun in and out of the holster several times. Shortly after midnight, Spector finally allowed Sacks and Henderson to leave his house. No charges were ever filed in connection with this incident.

5. *Spector's 2003 "Terrorist Treats" at Starbucks*
   In November 2003, nine months after the Clarkson killing, Spector walked into Starbucks coffee house on Fair Oaks Avenue in South Pasadena. Mr. Spector, who was reportedly intoxicated, shouted at the manager "Where's the pisser in this place?" The manager directed him to the men's room. Mr. Spector used the men's room, then walked outside of Starbucks.

   John Borowicz was seated outside Starbucks with his friends Andre and Art. As Spector walked out of Starbucks, Andre stood up and said to Spector,

"You're Phil Spector." Andre asked Spector to sit down and join them for coffee. Spector told them, "You s***, this interview isn't authorized," and "You fat f***, I'm gonna go get my gun and blow you fat fu*** away." Spector's driver approached Spector and walked him back to the black Mercedes sedan parked in front of Starbucks. The driver and Spector argued at the rear door of the Mercedes before Spector got into the back seat. The driver got behind the wheel, backed the Mercedes out of the parking stall and eventually left.

6. *Prior Firearm Incidents with Women*

DIANNE OGDEN (1988)

Dianne Ogden dated Mr. Spector several times in 1982. On one occasion they had a late dinner and she followed him to his home. He had been drinking at the restaurant and was slurring his words. When she said she had to go home, he locked the bars that secured the back door shut so she could not leave. She got angry and he became jovial and let her out of the house after an hour. Ogden later became his paid personal assistant. In 1988, she accompanied him home after a dinner date. At approximately 2 A.M., she indicated she wanted to leave. He pointed a pistol at her and touched the muzzle of the weapon to her skin. He yelled profanities at her. On another occasion when she attempted to leave, Spector exited the room carrying what Ogden described as an Uzi-type assault rifle. He chased her with the rifle and banged on the car windows and doors. None of these incidents was reported to the police.

MELISSA GROSVENOR (1991)

Melissa Grosvenor dated Spector for more than a year around 1991. Spector invited her to California, but sent only a one-way ticket, which concerned her. After she arrived they went to dinner and then to Spector's house. When she said she wanted to go home, he left the room and returned with a gun and pointed it at her. She was sitting in a chair crying, and eventually she fell asleep. The next day, Spector tapped her on the leg and asked if she wanted to go to breakfast. She agreed. After breakfast he asked her whether she wanted to leave and she said she did. He gave her a ticket to return to her home in New York.

DOROTHY MELVIN (1993)

Between 1989 and 1993, Dorothy Melvin dated Mr. Spector. Over the Fourth of July weekend in 1993, Melvin drove to Spector's home in Pasadena. They spent the evening inside his home. Mr. Spector drank alcohol, but Ms. Melvin did not. Melvin fell asleep and awoke to find Mr. Spector outside pointing a gun at her car. She left the house and asked him what he was doing and he told her to get the f*** back in the house. He pointed the gun at her. He struck her in the face with the handgun. He told her to take her clothes off and she refused. He again hit her with the gun. He went through her purse and accused her of stealing things from his home. He told her to get the f*** out of the house. She ran to her car and attempted to drive away. As she was leaving, she heard footsteps coming after her and heard the pump of a shotgun. He then went inside and unlocked the gate to the street. After she left she called the Pasadena Police Department. She went back to Spector's house with police to retrieve her handbag. He was handcuffed because he was belligerent. She chose not to press charges because she was concerned about bad publicity for herself and her employer, comedian Joan Rivers. He later left threatening phone messages on her answering machine.

STEPHANIE JENNINGS (1995)
Stephanie Jennings met Mr. Spector when she was working as a photographer at a music awards ceremony. She dated Spector for more than a year. He invited her to join him in California for a weekend. After she spent the evening at his home, he became angry with her. He refused to let her leave his house. She spoke with his assistant who told her to "wait it out." He eventually drove her back to her hotel.

On another occasion, he invited her to join him at a ceremony where he was inducted into the Rock and Roll Hall of Fame. She was staying in a separate room at the Carlyle Hotel and, after a night of drinking, Mr. Spector's bodyguard came to her room between 3 A.M. and 4 A.M. and said that Mr. Spector wanted her in his room. When she declined, he arrived at her room and slapped and shoved her. Spector left and then returned to the room with a gun which he pointed at her. She called 911 and the police arrived at the hotel. She indicated that she just wanted to leave, and the hotel manager gave her cab and train fare to get back to Philadelphia. She saw Mr. Spector socially after this incident. Spector left threatening messages on her answering machine later after she did not attend his birthday party.

DEBRA STRAND (1999)
In 1999, Debra Strand attended a Christmas party in Bel Air with her boyfriend, John Silberman. Spector was also in attendance at the party. Strand and Silberman left the party and returned to Silberman's home. Spector and his bodyguard also went to Silberman's house. Spector appeared to Strand to be intoxicated. Strand came out of the house's bathroom and saw Spector in the foyer of the house. Spector was flicking cigar ashes on Silberman's golden retriever, Dolly. Strand approached Sector and demanded that Spector leave the dog alone. Spector pulled a handgun out of his jacket and placed the muzzle of the weapon against her right cheek. Spector asked Strand, "how does this make you feel, bitch?" Strand was terrified that Spector might shoot her. Mr. Spector put the gun away, and his bodyguard led him away. She did not report the incident to the police. She was told by other people that Spector was very powerful in the music industry.

After the initial motion *in limine*, the State of California filed an additional motion *in limine* to include testimony of two additional women. The following sets forth the facts of those two incidents:

DEVRA ROBITAILLE (mid '70s and mid '80s)
Devra Robitaille worked for Warner Brothers in the 1970s. She later accepted a position as the Administrative Director for Warner-Spector Records, working directly for Mr. Spector. She dated Sector for approximately one year. On one occasion she was the last to leave a party at Spector's house. He had been drinking. She said she wanted to go home and he said no. He pointed a gun at her head, and said, "If you leave I'll blow your f***ing head off." Eventually he let her out. After that the relationship went back to platonic and professional. In the mid-eighties she again went to work for Spector. After a party, again, she tried to leave and he threatened her with a gun.

NORMA KEMPER (1996)
Norma Kemper was Mr. Spector's assistant for four years, from 1996 until 2000. She was never romantically involved with him. At dinner one evening, Mr. Spector attempted to kiss her. When she told him to stop, he opened up his jacket to reveal a shoulder holster and gun. He stated "you know, I could kill you right now." She stated that whenever Mr. Spector had alcohol he became quite mean.

Questions

404-7 If Mr. Spector's defense at trial was that the gun went off accidentally, may the government introduce into evidence Mr. Spector's history of gun violence?

404-8 If Mr. Spector's defense at trial was that the gun went off accidentally, may the government introduce into evidence Mr. Spector's alleged possession of unregistered firearms?

404-9 Should the prior incidents involving the brandishing of a firearm be allowed into evidence? Why or why not?

404-10 Judge Fidler ruled that the testimony of five of the women listed above (Ogden, Grosvenor, Melvin, Jennings, and Robitaille) was admissible under California Evidence Code Section 1101, which provides as follows:

(a) Except as provided in this section and in Sections 1102, 1103, 1108, and 1109, evidence of a person's character or a trait of his or her character (whether in the form of an opinion, evidence of reputation, or evidence of specific instances of his or her conduct) is inadmissible when offered to prove his or her conduct on a specified occasion. (b) Nothing in this section prohibits the admission of evidence that a person committed a crime, civil wrong, or other act when relevant to prove some fact (such as motive, opportunity, intent, preparation, plan, knowledge, identity, absence of mistake or accident, or whether a defendant in a prosecution for an unlawful sexual act or attempted unlawful sexual act did not reasonably and in good faith believe that the victim consented) other than his or her disposition to commit such an act. (c) Nothing in this section affects the admissibility of evidence offered to support or attack the credibility of a witness.

Was Judge Fidler correct in his ruling?

404-11   Why do you believe Judge Fidler ruled as inadmissible the testimony of Ms. Strand and Ms. Kemper?

404-12   Would the testimony of five or all seven of the women be admissible under the Federal Rules of Evidence Rule 404(b) prior bad acts?

404-13   If the testimony of prior bad acts is admissible under Rule 404(b), should it be excluded nevertheless under Rule 403?

Rule 405. Methods of Proving Character

(a) Reputation or opinion.

In all cases in which evidence of character or a trait of character of a person is admissible, proof may be made by testimony as to reputation or by testimony in the form of an opinion. On cross-examination, inquiry is allowable into relevant specific instances of conduct.

(b) Specific instances of conduct.

In cases in which character or a trait of character of a person is an essential element of a charge, claim, or defense, proof may also be made of specific instances of that person's conduct.

This is really a rule of procedure, not substance. In the event character is admissible (under Rule 404), how may a party prove the character trait? There are three possibilities — opinion, reputation, and specific instances of conduct. The Advisory Committee considered "specific instances" the most convincing evidence. See Advisory Committee Notes to Rule 405. On the other hand, the Committee also considered it the most prejudicial.

Suppose the prosecution is using character of gun violence to show the absence of mistake or accident. Lin is charged with murdering Chen. Lin defends herself by claiming that she was cleaning her gun and it accidentally discharged a bullet, which killed Chen. The prosecution could attempt to prove this character trait by the following three methods:

1.   Juan testifies that in his opinion, Lin is a violent person (opinion).
2.   Eric testifies that Lin has a reputation for being violent (reputation).
3.   Sarah testifies that two months prior to the charged incident, Lin pointed a gun at her and threatened to kill her (specific instance).

Is the third type of evidence the most convincing? If so, is it also the most prejudicial? Clearly, the Advisory Committee believed so. Therefore, the use of specific instance evidence is significantly limited.

Specific instance evidence is admissible on cross-examination of a witness. It is also admissible if character is an "essential element of a charge, claim or defense." If a character witness is called at trial to render his or her opinion, or to prove the reputation of an individual, specific instances of conduct may be inquired into on cross-examination. Joe is on trial for assaulting Amy. Joe calls Paul as a character witness in his defense. Paul testifies that Joe is one of the most peaceful persons Joe has ever met (opinion). Paul further testifies that Joe is known as being peaceable and kind (reputation). Now the prosecution may ask Paul whether he has ever heard that Joe previously was arrested for assaulting Carl (specific instances on cross-examination).

One may wish to take 405(b) and run with it. Its use is actually quite limited. It is only allowed if the character trait *itself* is an issue in the case. When would a character trait itself be the issue in the case? If someone is accused of defamation, truth may be his or her defense. Consider a situation in which Mary is accused of defaming Ben. Mary stated that Ben, a senator, "is the most corrupt politician ever!" How would Mary defend herself? She would have to prove that Ben indeed is corrupt. Specific instances of Ben's corruption would be admissible. Character is "in issue" in only rare instances, such as defamation, entrapment, libel, and slander cases. The Ninth Circuit Court of Appeals has held that "the relevant question should be: would proof, or failure of proof, of the character trait by itself actually satisfy an element of the charge, claim, or defense? If not, then character is not essential and evidence should be limited to opinion or reputation." *United States v. Keiser*, 57 F.3d 847, 856 (9th Cir. 1995).

Although the use of specific instances is strictly limited under Rule 405, it seems the rule is more honored in the breach, apparently due to the lack of an objection. Bear in mind also that Rule 404(b) says "acts."

Questions

405-1 Was the testimony of the five female witnesses discussed in Rule 404 above based upon opinion, reputation, or specific instances?

405-2 Would the testimony of the five women discussed in Rule 404 have been admissible under 405?

405-3 Would the testimony be admissible under the California Code provision cited above?

Rule 406. Habit; Routine Practice

Evidence of the habit of a person or of the routine practice of an organization, whether corroborated or not and regardless of the presence of eyewitnesses, is relevant to prove that the conduct of the person or organization on a particular occasion was in conformity with the habit or routine practice.

Character evidence is generally not admissible in evidence, but habit evidence is. What is the difference between character and habit? In making a distinction, the Advisory Committee cited to *McCormick on Evidence* as follows:

> Character may be thought of as the sum of one's habits through doubtless it is more than this. But unquestionably the uniformity of one's response to habit is far greater than the consistency with which one's conduct conforms to character or disposition. Even though character comes in only exceptionally as evidence of an act, surely any sensible man in investigating whether X did a particular act would be greatly helped in his inquiry by evidence as to whether he was in the habit of doing it. McCormick on Evidence, Sec. 162, p. 341, as cited in the Advisory Committee Notes to Rule 406.

Habit is thought of as a regular response to a specific stimulus — like the famous Pavlov's dogs (dogs drool at the sound of a bell). Proof of regularity is required. Four prior convictions for public intoxication over a three and one-half year period was not enough regularity to establish a man was intoxicated when run over by a train. *Reyes v. Missouri Pac. R. Co.*, 589 F.2d 791 (5th Cir. 1979). If one could show a defendant woke up each and every morning and drank a shot of whiskey, that would rise to the level of a habit.

Question

406-1   Would Mr. Spector's prior incidences of gun violence rise to the level of a habit?

Rule 410. Inadmissibility of Pleas, Plea Discussions, and Related Statements

Except as otherwise provided in this rule, evidence of the following is not, in any civil or criminal proceeding, admissible against the defendant who made the plea or was a participant in the plea discussions:

(1) a plea of guilty which was later withdrawn;
(2) a plea of nolo contendere;
(3) any statement made in the course of any proceedings under Rule 11 of the Federal Rules of Criminal Procedure or comparable state procedure regarding either of the foregoing pleas; or
(4) any statement made in the course of plea discussions with an attorney for the prosecuting authority which do not result in a plea of guilty or which result in a plea of guilty later withdrawn.

However, such a statement is admissible (i) in any proceeding wherein another statement made in the course of the same plea or plea discussions has been introduced and the statement ought in fairness be considered contemporaneously with it, or (ii) in a criminal proceeding for perjury or false statement if the statement was made by the defendant under oath, on the record and in the presence of counsel.

On May 29, 2007, the defense filed a motion in the Spector trial to prevent any mention of conversations between Robert Shapiro (then counsel for Phil Spector) and Patrick Dixon (Head Deputy of the Major Crimes Division of the Los Angeles County District Attorney's Office) that occurred on September 26, 2003.

Questions

410-1   Is the conversation mentioned in the defendant's motion inadmissible in a later trial?

410-2   Suppose Mr. Spector pleaded guilty to second-degree murder. Would this plea be admissible in the later civil case for wrongful death?

410-3   Is the guilty verdict delivered by the jury against Mr. Spector admissible in the later civil case for wrongful death?

Rule 412. Sex Offense Cases; Relevance of Alleged Victim's Past Sexual Behavior or Alleged Sexual Predisposition

(a) Evidence generally inadmissible.
   The following evidence is not admissible in any civil or criminal proceeding involving alleged sexual misconduct except as provided in subdivisions (b) and (c):
   (1) Evidence offered to prove that any alleged victim engaged in other sexual behavior.
   (2) Evidence offered to prove any alleged victim's sexual predisposition.

(b) Exceptions.
   (1) In a criminal case, the following evidence is admissible, if otherwise admissible under these rules:
      (A) evidence of specific instances of sexual behavior by the alleged victim offered to prove that a person other than the accused was the source of semen, injury, or other physical evidence;
      (B) evidence of specific instances of sexual behavior by the alleged victim with respect to the person accused of the sexual misconduct offered by the accused to prove consent or by the prosecution; and
      (C) evidence the exclusion of which would violate the constitutional rights of the defendant.
   (2) In a civil case, evidence offered to prove the sexual behavior or sexual predisposition of any alleged victim is admissible if it is otherwise admissible under these rules and its probative value substantially outweighs the danger of harm to any victim and of unfair prejudice to any party. Evidence of an alleged victim's reputation is admissible only if it has been placed in controversy by the alleged victim.

(c) Procedure to determine admissibility.
   (1) A party intending to offer evidence under subdivision (b) must—
      (A) file a written motion at least 14 days before trial specifically describing the evidence and stating the purpose for which it is offered unless the court,

> for good cause requires a different time for filing or permits filing during trial; and
>
> (B) serve the motion on all parties and notify the alleged victim or, when appropriate, the alleged victim's guardian or representative.
>
> (2) Before admitting evidence under this rule the court must conduct a hearing in camera and afford the victim and parties a right to attend and be heard. The motion, related papers, and the record of the hearing must be sealed and remain under seal unless the court orders otherwise.

Rules 412 through 415 are special rules passed by the United States Legislature some time after the Federal Rules were adopted. The 404 rules do not apply to these particular circumstances. The first rule, Rule 412, applies to the sexual character of the *victim*. The other three rules, Rules 413, 414, and 415, apply to the sexual character of the *defendant*. Rule 412 has provisions for both *criminal and civil cases*. Rule 413 applies to *criminal sexual assault cases*. Rule 414 applies to *criminal child molestation cases* and Rule 415 applies to *civil sexual assault and child molestation cases*.

Rule 412 is referred to as the "Rape Shield Law" and it was adopted in 1978 as part of the Privacy Protection for Rape Victims Act. Congress believed that rape victims were often harassed and humiliated at trial. During congressional hearings reports were cited that many rapes went unreported, possibility due to this harassment and humiliation. Therefore, a victim's prior sexual behavior is generally inadmissible. Note that congressional action in directly passing evidence rules has been extremely limited. Generally rule changes originate with the Advisory Committee. In 1994, the Rule was amended by the Advisory Committee to clarify some provisions of the rule. In the Committee Notes they indicate that "sexual behavior" includes a victim's mode of dress, speech, or lifestyle. For example, a defendant may not introduce evidence that a victim has posed nude in a magazine in a sexual harassment case. See *Burns v. McGregor Electronic Industries, Inc.*, 989 F.2d 959, 962 (8th Cir. 1993), cited in the Advisory Committee Notes to Rule 412.

In order to protect the defendant's rights, there are exceptions to the general rule of disallowance. The exceptions are divided for criminal versus civil cases. For example, if a defendant claims that another person was the source of the injury, he or she may introduce evidence to prove this point. He or she may also introduce evidence of prior instances of sexual behavior specifically with him or her — typically in a case in which the defendant asserts the sexual "misconduct" alleged was consensual. Rule 412(b)(2) is actually superfluous. Constitutional Rules always trump the rules of evidence. However, this provision was added no doubt in response to the *Olden v. Kentucky* case. *Olden v. Kentucky*, 488 U.S. 227 (1988). In that case, the Supreme Court held that a defendant was constitutionally entitled to introduce the past sexual history of a woman (her cohabitation with another man) to show bias.

Questions

412-1 May the defense call Jennifer Hayes-Riedl, a self-professed friend of Ms. Clarkson, to testify that Lana Clarkson "dated everyone and his dog"?

412-2 The defense would like to introduce into evidence Lana Clarkson's diary. Do you believe this is admissible?

Rule 413. Evidence of Similar Crimes in Sexual Assault Cases

(a) In a criminal case in which the defendant is accused of an offense of sexual assault, evidence of the defendant's commission of another offense or offenses of sexual assault is admissible, and may be considered for its bearing on any matter to which it is relevant.

(b) In a case in which the Government intends to offer evidence under this rule, the attorney for the Government shall disclose the evidence to the defendant, including statements of witnesses or a summary of the substance of any testimony that is expected to be offered, at least fifteen days before the scheduled date of trial or at such later time as the court may allow for good cause.

(c) This rule shall not be construed to limit the admission or consideration of evidence under any other rule.

(d) For purposes of this rule and Rule 415, "offense of sexual assault" means a crime under Federal law or the law of a State (as defined in section 513 of title 18, United States Code) that involved —

    (1) any conduct proscribed by chapter 109A of title 18, United States Code;

    (2) contact, without consent, between any part of the defendant's body or an object and the genitals or anus of another person;

    (3) contact, without consent, between the genitals or anus of the defendant and any part of another person's body;

    (4) deriving sexual pleasure or gratification from the infliction of death, bodily injury, or physical pain on another person; or

    (5) an attempt or conspiracy to engage in conduct described in paragraphs (1)-(4).

Rules 413 through 415 were also passed by Congress by procedures that differ from those of the other Federal Rules. These were passed by the Violent Crime Control and Law Enforcement Act of 1994, effective in 1995. Interestingly, the Judicial Conference opposed Rules 413 through 415. The Chief Justice of the United States is the presiding officer of the Judicial Conference. Membership is comprised of the chief judge of each judicial circuit, the Chief Judge of the Court of International Trade, and a district judge from each regional judicial circuit. Source: www.uscourts.gov. The Conference indicated that it unanimously opposed the new rules (and indicated that the only support for the new rules came from the Justice Department). Congress did not follow the Conference's recommendations. Congress cited to a report entitled "Evidence of Propensity and Probability in Sex Offense Cases and Other Cases" by David Karp of the United States Justice Department. Congress believes that these cases are different — the perpetrators have "a sexual or sadosexual interest in children that simply does not exist in ordinary people." Further, Congress specifically stated the following:

> Evidence of offenses for which the defendant has not previously been prosecuted or convicted will be admissible, as well as evidence of prior convictions. No time limit is imposed on the uncharged offenses for which evidence may be admitted; as a practical matter, evidence of other sex offenses by the defendant is often probative and properly admitted, notwithstanding very substantial lapses of time in relation to the charged offense or offenses.

Congressional testimony of Representative Susan Molinari, August 21, 1994, cited in the Advisory Committee Notes to Rule 413.

Question

413-1 If a Sheriff's Criminalist (Steve Renteria) testifies that Phil Spector's DNA was found on Ms. Clarkson's left breast, may the prosecution offer into evidence Mr. Spector's alleged past sexual misconduct?

ARTICLE V. PRIVILEGES

Rule 501. General Rule

Except as otherwise required by the Constitution of the United States or provided by Act of Congress or in rules prescribed by the Supreme Court pursuant to statutory authority, the privilege of a witness, person, government, State, or political subdivision thereof shall be governed by the principles of the common law as they may be interpreted by the courts of the United States in the light of reason and experience. However, in civil actions and proceedings, with respect to an element of a claim or defense as to which State law supplies the rule of decision, the privilege of a witness, person, government, State, or political subdivision thereof shall be determined in accordance with State law.

Rule 501 of the Federal Rules of Evidence sets forth the general rules of privilege. The rule is simple. The rules of privilege are "governed by the principles of the common law as they may be interpreted by the courts of the United States in the light of reason and experience." It is a rule that essentially provides that we should look to case law.

The process of codifying rules of evidence began in 1811 with Jeremy Bentham's offer to President Madison to "codify the American common law." Charles Alan Wright & Kenneth W. Graham, Jr., *Federal Practice and Procedure* (Wright & Graham), Sec. 5005, at 62. Many attempts were made at codification throughout the years, but it was not until the adoption of the Uniform Rules of Evidence by the American Law Institute in 1953 that strides were made toward codification.

The drafting of the Federal Rules of Evidence as we know them today began in 1958. In 1961, the Judicial Conference authorized a committee to investigate this possibility, and United States Supreme Court Justice Earl Warren appointed the committee. Wright & Graham, Sec. 5005, at 92. Most of the work of the Committee was done by Professor Cleary, who later testified at a House subcommittee meeting that privileges "often operated as blockades to the quest for truth." Edward J. Imwinkelried, *The New Wigmore: A Treatise on Evidence*, Sec. 4.2.1(b), at 153 and Wright & Graham, Sec. 5006, at 99.

The original Privilege Rules (Article 5) as submitted to Congress listed 13 separate provisions. According to the Report of the House Committee on the Judiciary, "nine of those rules defined specific non-constitutional privileges which the federal courts must recognize (i.e., required reports, lawyer-client, psychotherapist-patient, husband-wife, communications to clergymen, political vote, trade secrets, secrets of state and other official information, and identity of informer)." These rules were never adopted. "The Committee amended Article V to eliminate all of the Court's specific Rules on privileges. Instead, the Committee, through a single Rule 501, left the law of privileges in its present state and further provided that privileges shall continue to be developed by the courts of the United States under a uniform standard applicable both in civil and criminal cases." Report of the House Committee on the Judiciary. What happened between the nine separately delineated privileges rule, and the general "governed by common law" text of Rule 501? In a word, Watergate.

The years 1972 and 1973 were significant for their effect on privilege law. Wright & Graham. On June 17, 1972, the Watergate burglars were caught and arrested as they attempted to bug Democratic National Committee headquarters at the Watergate hotel in Washington, D.C. On June 3, 1973, John Dean, the White House Counsel, told the Watergate investigators that he and President Nixon had discussed the cover-up at least 35 times. On July 23, 1973, President Nixon refused to turn over the presidential tape recordings he made while in office and cited executive privilege. In the landmark case *United States v. Nixon*, the U.S. Supreme Court found that the executive privilege was not absolute, and it ordered Nixon to turn over the tapes and records. *United States v. Nixon*, 418 U.S. 683 (July 24, 1974).

The Watergate events had a definite impact on the privilege rules. Senator Sam Ervin was both Chairman of the Watergate Committee and the Chair of the Senate Judiciary Committee. Imwinkelried, *The New Wigmore*, at 165 and 176. He introduced Senate Bill 583 in order to delay the effective date of the rules that had been promulgated by the Supreme Court. A similar provision was passed in the House, and a report prepared at that time indicated that the delay was intended "to promote the separation of constitutional powers." The congressional debates on the rules contained numerous references to the Watergate controversy. Edward J. Imwinkelried, *Whether the Federal Rules of Evidence Should Be Conceived as a Perpetual Index Code: Blindness Is Worse Than Myopia*, 40 Wm. & Mary L. Rev. 1595, 1601 (1999).

On June 28, 1973, the Judiciary Committee released a "Committee Print of the Federal Rules." The House amended the earlier privilege provisions, and the nine specific privilege rules were eliminated and replaced with a provision almost identical to Federal Rule of Evidence 501. The Committee Print was adopted by the House and the Senate and was signed by President Ford on January 2, 1975, to take effect on July 1, 1975.

What privileges have been developed through Common Law? The following have been recognized by federal courts:

1. *Attorney-Client*
2. *Attorney Work Product*
3. *Spousal Privileges (Testimonial and Confidential Communication)*
4. *Psychotherapist-Patient*
5. *Clergy-Parishioner*
6. *Executive Privilege*
7. *Reporter Privilege (most federal courts)*

Attorney-Client Privilege

The attorney-client privilege began not as a protection for a client, but as "obligations of honor among gentlemen" John Henry Wigmore, *A Treatise on the System of Evidence in Trials at Common Law* Sec. 2286, at 3187-88. It was believed that only a dishonorable lawyer would reveal a client's secrets. The privilege belonged to the attorney, not the client (as is the case today).

John Henry Wigmore became America's foremost authority on evidence law. Wigmore developed "four fundamental conditions" of privilege law, which are the following:

1. The communications must originate in a confidence that they will not be disclosed;
2. This element of confidentiality must be essential to the full and satisfactory maintenance of the relation between the parties;
3. The relation must be one which in the opinion of the community ought to be sedulously fostered; and
4. The injury that would inure to the relation by the disclosure of the communications must be greater than the benefit thereby gained for the correct disposal of litigation.

A draft of the rules was submitted for comment in 1969, with Article V of that draft containing the privilege rules. One of the delineated rules was the attorney-client privilege (5-03). In a March 1971 revised draft, Rule 5-03 became 503, and the drafters added a fourth section. Edward J. Imwinkelried, *The New Wigmore: A Treatise on Evidence*, and Wright & Graham. The following is a text of the attorney-client privilege rule at this point:

> A client has a privilege to refuse to disclose and to prevent any other person from disclosing confidential communications (1) between himself or his representative and his lawyer or his lawyer's representative, or (2) between his lawyer and the lawyer's representative, or (3) made for the purpose of facilitating the rendition of professional legal services to the client, by him or his lawyer to a lawyer representing another in a matter of common interest, or (4) between representatives of the client or between the client and a representative of the client.

The purpose of the attorney-client privilege is "to encourage full and frank communication between attorneys and their clients and thereby promote broader public interests in the observance of law and administration of justice." *Upjohn Co. v. United States*, 449 U.S. 383, 389 (1981). The lawyer must be aware of all the facts and circumstances in order to adequately represent his or her client. Upjohn, citing to *Trammel v. United States*, 445 U.S. 40, 51 (1980).

As mentioned above, today the privilege belongs to the client, and the attorney is expected to safeguard it on behalf of the client. Utmost candor between the attorney and the client is absolutely essential if a client is to have effective assistance of counsel. *Greater Newburyport Clamshell Alliance v. Public Service Company of New Hampshire*, 838 F.2d 13, 21 (1st Cir. 1988).

On the other hand, because it "impedes full and free discovery of the truth," the attorney-client privilege is to be strictly construed. *Weil v. Investment Indicators, Research and Management, Inc.*, 647 F.2d 18, 24 (9th Cir. 1981). The burden of proving that the privilege applies is on the party asserting the privilege. Privileges "are not favored," even if they have constitutional roots. *Herbert v. Lando*, 441 U.S. 153, 175 (1979). Courts are to confine the privilege to its "narrowest possible limits consistent with the logic of its principle." *In re Grand Jury Proceedings*, 727 F.2d 1352 (4th Cir. 1984). Without limitations, the privilege would "engulf all manner of services performed for (sic) the lawyer that are not now, and should not be, summarily excluded from the adversary process." *In re Lindsey*, 158 F.3d 1263, 1281 (D.C. Cir. 1998), *cert. den.* 525 U.S. 996 (1998), entitled *Office of the President v. Office of Independent Counsel*. Bruce R. Lindsey was an attorney in the Office of President Clinton.

The Attorney Work-Product Privilege

The attorney work-product privilege is not actually a privilege — it constitutes immunity from discovery under the Federal Rules of Civil Procedure. Materials prepared in anticipation of litigation, including witness statements, are not subject to discovery and are protected by the attorney work-product privilege. *Hickman v. Taylor*, 329 U.S. 495 (1947). In *Hickman v. Taylor*, the Supreme Court stated the following:

> Proper preparation of a client's case demands that he assemble information, sift what he considers to be the relevant from the irrelevant facts, prepare his legal theories, and plan his strategy without undue and needless interference. . . . This work is reflected, of course, in interviews, statements, memoranda, correspondence, briefs, mental impressions, personal beliefs, and countless other tangible and intangible ways. . . . Were such materials open to opposing counsel on mere demand, much of what is now put down in writing would remain unwritten.

This holding has been incorporated into the Federal Rules of Civil Procedure at Rule 26(b) (3), which states the following:

(A) *Documents and Tangible Things*. Ordinarily, a party may not discover documents and tangible things that are prepared in anticipation of litigation or for trial by or for another party or its representative (including the other party's attorney, consultant, surety, indemnitor, insurer, or agent). But, subject to Rule 26(b)(4), those materials may be discovered if:
  (i) they are otherwise discoverable under Rule 26(b)(1); and
  (ii) the party shows that it has substantial need for the materials to prepare its case and cannot, without undue hardship, obtain their substantial equivalent by other means.

(B) *Protection Against Disclosure*. If the court orders discovery of those materials, it must protect against disclosure of the mental impressions, conclusions, opinions, or legal theories of a party's attorney or other representative concerning the litigation.

As is apparent from the rule, the attorney work-product privilege is not absolute. If a party proves a "substantial need" for the materials that they are unable to otherwise obtain "without undue hardship," they are entitled to the material. However, even in this event, the attorney's actual "mental impressions, conclusions, opinions, or legal theories" are still immune from discovery. Thus, there is what some term a distinction between "ordinary" work product and "opinion" work product, the latter being more strictly protected from discovery. A similar work-product rule appears in the Federal Rules of Criminal Procedure, at Rule 16. Although it is not a true "privilege" according to the Supreme Court, it operates similarly to one, as in Grand Jury proceedings. See, for example, *In re Grand Jury Subpoena*, 599 F.2d 504, 509 (2nd Cir. 1979).

Only material that is "prepared in anticipation of litigation" is subject to the attorney work-product privilege. In *Coastal States Gas Corp. v. Department of Energy*, the U.S. Court of Appeals for the D.C. Circuit indicated that the privilege/immunity does not attach until "at the very least some articulable claim, likely to lead to litigation" has arisen. 617 F.2d 854 (D.C. Cir. 1980). The party claiming that the immunity applies has the burden to show that the material is protected by the work-product privilege. *Zaentz v. Commissioner*, 73 T.C. 469, 475 (1979). Typically, the party claiming the privilege will submit a privilege log to the court to document the author's name, addressee's name, and a brief statement of the subject matter of each document. The court may then choose to examine the documents *in camera*. The burden then shifts to the opposing party to prove the "substantial need" and "undue hardship" in order to overcome the privilege. *Kent Corp. v. NLRB*, 530 F.2d 612, 623-624 (5th Cir. 1976). "Opinion" work-product material has "nearly absolute immunity" from discovery. *In re Murphy*, 560 F.2d 326, 336 (8th Cir. 1977).

Spousal Privileges

There are actually two spousal privileges — one is for confidential communications and the other is a testimonial privilege. The *Confidential Communication Privilege* is held by both spouses. It covers only statements made during the pendency of the marriage, and applies only to communications that are made in confidence ("pillow talk"). The *Testimonial Spousal Privilege* applies during the marriage, but may apply to statements made before the parties married. The purpose of the testimonial privilege is to protect the sanctity of marriage, so that one spouse may not be forced to testify against the other spouse. The spouse called to testify holds the privilege.

If Bob and Susan have a conversation in which Bob admits he murdered Jed, and later Bob and Susan marry, the confidential communication privilege would not apply — it applies only to confidential statements made *while* married. On the other hand, Susan may refuse to testify against Bob about this statement — because they are currently married (the testimonial privilege). Interestingly, the United States Supreme Court held that if Susan wishes to testify, she may. See *Trammel v. United States*, 445 U.S. 40 (1980). Bob could not prevent Susan from revealing the conversation. The Court reasoned that if an individual was willing to testify against his or her spouse, the marriage is already beyond saving. If Bob made the statement while married to Susan and it was said in confidence, Susan may not reveal the conversation — Bob may prevent her from doing so, as he holds the confidential communication privilege.

Many privilege issues were raised by the *Spector* case. *First*, Mr. Spector discharged and later sued his first attorney Robert Shapiro. *Second*, one of Mr. Spector's attorneys was called as a witness to describe an event she observed during the investigation in this case. *Third*, Michelle Blaine alleged that Mr. Spector contemplated their marriage so that her testimony would be protected by the spousal testimonial privilege.

Mr. Spector was arrested on February 3, 2003. At 6:09 A.M. he retained a lawyer, Robert Shapiro, while he was in police custody. Mr. Shapiro had become famous for his representation of O.J. Simpson (Mr. Shapiro was a member of the "dream team"), and he had become Mr. Spector's friend. Mr. Shapiro arrived at the jail at approximately noon and Mr. Spector was released on bail at 7:00 P.M. Four days later, Mr. Spector signed a written agreement with Mr. Shapiro for Mr. Shapiro to represent him in connection with his arrest. In January 2004, Mr. Spector fired Mr. Shapiro and on July 1, 2004, Mr. Spector sued Mr. Shapiro for the return of his $1 million retainer paid to Mr. Shapiro. Mr. Spector alleged that Mr. Shapiro took advantage of him when he was in a weakened state and was "laboring under a tremendous amount of mental stress." Bruce Cutler, Mr. Spector's attorney for the criminal trial, called Mr. Shapiro's actions "financial rape" of Mr. Spector.

Mr. Shapiro took Mr. Spector's deposition on July 19, 2005. The State of California subsequently served a subpoena duces tecum (subpoena to produce documents) for a copy of the transcript and a DVD of this deposition. Mr. Spector asserted that the deposition was protected by the attorney-client privilege. At the time of the deposition, Mr. Spector had not sought a protective order and had not sought a confidentiality agreement. In January 2006, Judge Fidler ruled that portions of the deposition were to be made available to the prosecution and the public.

In *Hunt v. Blackburn*, 128 U.S. 464, 470 (1888) the Supreme Court addressed the issue of the waiver of the attorney-client privilege in the following manner:

> The rule which places the seal of secrecy upon communications between client and attorney is founded upon the necessity, in the interest and administration of justice, of the aid of persons having knowledge of the law and skilled in its practice, which assistance can only be safely and readily availed of when free from the consequences or the apprehension of disclosure. But the privilege is that of the client alone, and no rule prohibits the latter from divulging his own secrets. **And if the client has voluntarily waived the privilege, it cannot be insisted on to close the mouth of the attorney. When Mrs. Blackburn entered upon a line of defense which involved what transpired between herself and Mr. Weatherford, and respecting which she testified, she waived her right to object to his giving his own account of the matter.**

Sara Caplan, an attorney in the first trial for Mr. Spector, was held in contempt of court by Judge Fidler on June 18, 2007, for refusing to testify about a missing piece of evidence. She was ordered jailed, but the judge allowed a stay of the order to allow her to immediately appeal his order. A law clerk had earlier alleged that Ms. Caplan had picked up a piece of evidence at Mr. Spector's residence on the morning of his arrest. In surprising previous testimony, Ms. Caplan had indicated that renowned forensic expert Henry Lee (an expert for O.J. Simpson at the O.J. Simpson trial) picked up the piece of evidence and put it in a vial. She testified that she never saw the object or knew what happened to it. The State alleged that Mr. Lee found a fingernail and picked it up to shield it from the police investigators.

Ms. Caplan later refused to answer questions and cited the attorney-client privilege and her confidential duty to her client. After being held in contempt she ultimately answered questions and the judge determined that Henry Lee had indeed taken some piece of evidence from the scene. He decided not to hold Lee in contempt, as there was conflicting evidence and Lee was located outside of the country.

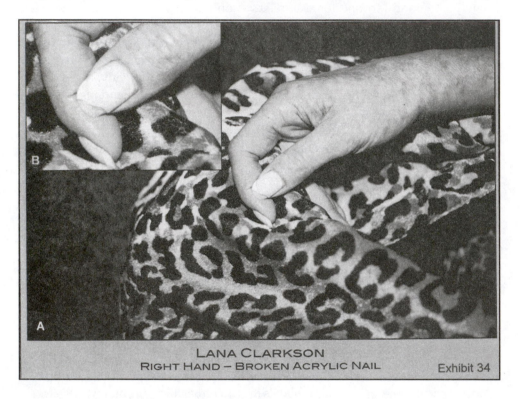

LANA CLARKSON
RIGHT HAND – BROKEN ACRYLIC NAIL
Exhibit 34

In September 2005, Mr. Spector filed a civil lawsuit against Michele Blaine, his former assistant. Michelle Blaine was the daughter of Hal Blaine, a legendary drummer and founder of the band, The Wrecking Crew. Mr. Blaine had previously worked on Mr. Spector's albums. Ms. Blaine worked for Spector for approximately four years and was in his employ when he was arrested. Mr. Spector later alleged that Ms. Blaine embezzled funds from his accounts and received an unauthorized loan to purchase a home. Ms. Blaine countersued for $5.25 million and alleged, among other things, sexual harassment. The lawsuit was settled when Ms. Blaine agreed to pay Mr. Spector $900,000. During the pendency of the civil lawsuit, Ms. Blaine alleged that Mr. Spector pressured her to marry him so that she would not be able to be called as a witness against him in his criminal trial.

Questions

501-1 When Mr. Spector sued Mr. Shapiro for the return of his $1 million retainer, did he waive the attorney-client privilege?

501-2 Was Ms. Caplan correct in her assertion of the attorney-client privilege?

501-3 If Ms. Blaine had married Mr. Spector, would she have been able to refuse to testify against him? Could Mr. Spector have prevented her from testifying?

Rule 502. Attorney-Client Privilege and Work Product; Limitations on Waiver

The following provisions apply, in the circumstances set out, to disclosure of a communication or information covered by the attorney-client privilege or work-product protection.

(a) Disclosure Made in a Federal Proceeding or to a Federal Office or Agency; Scope of a Waiver — When the disclosure is made in a Federal proceeding or to a Federal office or agency and waives the attorney-client privilege or work-product protection, the waiver extends to an undisclosed communication or information in a Federal or State proceeding only if:
   1. the waiver is intentional;
   2. the disclosed and undisclosed communications or information concern the same subject matter; and
   3. they ought in fairness to be considered together.

(b) Inadvertent Disclosure — When made in a Federal proceeding or to a Federal office or agency, the disclosure does not operate as a waiver in a Federal or State proceeding if:
   1. the disclosure is inadvertent;
   2. the holder of the privilege or protection took reasonable steps to prevent disclosure; and
   3. the holder promptly took reasonable steps to rectify the error, including (if applicable) following Federal Rule of Civil Procedure 26(b)(5)(B).

(c) Disclosure Made in a State Proceeding —
   When the disclosure is made in a State proceeding and is not the subject of a State-court order concerning waiver, the disclosure does not operate as a waiver in a Federal proceeding if the disclosure:
   1. would not be a waiver under this rule if it had been made in a Federal proceeding; or
   2. is not a waiver under the law of the State where the disclosure occurred.

(d) Controlling Effect of a Court Order —
   A Federal court may order that the privilege or protection is not waived by disclosure connected with the litigation pending before the court — in which event the disclosure is also not a waiver in any other Federal or State proceeding.

(e) Controlling Effect of a Party Agreement —
   An agreement on the effect of disclosure in a Federal proceeding is binding only on the parties to the agreement, unless it is incorporated into a court order.

(f) Controlling Effect of This Rule —
   Notwithstanding Rules 101 and 1101, this rule applies to State proceedings and to Federal court-annexed and Federal court-mandated arbitration proceedings, in the

circumstances set out in the rule. And notwithstanding Rule 501, this rule applies even if State law provides the rule of decision.

(g) Definitions —

In this rule:

1. "attorney-client privilege" means the protection that applicable law provides for confidential attorney-client communications; and
2. "work-product protection" means the protection that applicable law provides for tangible material (or its intangible equivalent) prepared in anticipation of litigation or for trial.

Rule 502 is a relatively new rule, added in 2008. According to the Advisory Committee Notes, it was added for the following two purposes:

1. to resolve "long-standing disputes" in the courts about the effect disclosures had on the attorney-client and work product privileges; and
2. to address the cost implicated in the protection of the attorney-client and work-product privileges, particularly in electronic discovery cases.

A law school graduate may begin his or her legal career performing "document review." This task is necessary in order for a client to respond to discovery requests. A lawyer must review the client's documents to see what documents are responsive to a discovery request. The lawyer will also be reviewing the documents in order to later claim the attorney-client or work-product privileges. This task is obviously labor-intensive and quite expensive. Many firms outsource this task, including sending the job overseas, particularly when the discovery documents are electronic. Attorneys must be ever vigilant to avoid the release of a document protected under a privilege. Prior to this Rule, if a document was inadvertently released, the privilege was waived — with respect to the entire subject matter of the released document. As litigation became more complex and an ever-increasing number of documents were being requested via discovery, lawyers were spending a great deal of time and money ensuring that no document or communication was disclosed inadvertently. Litigation costs due to the fear of inadvertent disclosure were increasing dramatically. Courts began to take notice. In *Hopson v. City of Baltimore*, the District Court for the District of Maryland stated the following, "electronic discovery may encompass millions of documents and to insist upon record-by-record pre-production privilege review on pain of subject matter waiver, would impose upon parties costs of production that bear no proportionality to what is at stake in the litigation," 232 F.R.D. 228 (D. Md. 2005), as cited in the Advisory Committee Note to Federal Rule of Evidence 502.

This new provision is meant to protect attorneys from an inadvertent disclosure disaster. Now "inadvertent disclosure of protected communications or information in connection with a federal proceeding or to a federal office or agency does not constitute a waiver if the holder took reasonable steps to prevent disclosure and also promptly took reasonable steps to rectify the error." Advisory Committee Notes to Rule 502.

ARTICLE VI. WITNESSES

Rule 601. General Rule of Competency

Every person is competent to be a witness except as otherwise provided in these rules. However, in civil actions and proceedings, with respect to an element of a claim or defense as to which State law supplies the rule of decision, the competency of a witness shall be determined in accordance with State law.

In the past, many individuals were prohibited from testifying. If one goes back far enough in history, nearly everyone was prohibited from testifying. At a later time, anyone with an interest in the lawsuit was kept from the stand. Later still only the elite were allowed to speak in court. Today, the rules are much less restrictive. Generally, provided one is able to differentiate truth from untruth, he or she is allowed to testify in court. It is the jury's duty to test the credibility of the witness.

Mr. Spector acknowledged in his deposition in the *Spector v. Shapiro* case that he had been prescribed and had taken five medications for years. He stated that the medications were for the symptoms of "manic depressiveness." In response to a question about his symptoms, he answered "no sleep, depression, mood changes, mood swings, hard to live with, hard to concentrate, hard — just hard — a hard time getting through life." He mentioned three of the medications — Prozac (antidepressant), Neurontin (anticonvulsant), and Klonopin (panic disorder). He was unable to recall the names of the other two medications.

Question

601-1 If called as a witness in this case, would Mr. Spector be competent to testify?

Rule 602. Lack of Personal Knowledge

A witness may not testify to a matter unless evidence is introduced sufficient to support a finding that the witness has personal knowledge of the matter. Evidence to prove personal knowledge may, but need not, consist of the witness' own testimony. This rule is subject to the provisions of Rule 703, relating to opinion testimony by expert witnesses.

This rule seems rather straightforward and obvious. No witness may testify unless they know, from personal knowledge, what they are talking about. Why in the world would an attorney call to the stand a witness who has no personal knowledge? Either the attorney does not understand the rules of evidence, or it's the best the attorney can do under the circumstances. Consider this: Mahmoud witnesses an accident — he sees a green car go through a red light and hit a pedestrian. He is quoted in a local newspaper. At trial, the pedestrian calls the editor of the local newspaper in order to testify about the accident. It may be that Mahmoud has died and the pedestrian is no longer able to call him as a witness. The next best thing is to call the newspaper editor. Will this be allowed under the Federal Rules of Evidence? No. The newspaper editor has no personal knowledge of the accident.

Rule 606. Competency of Juror as Witness

(a) At the trial.

A member of the jury may not testify as a witness before that jury in the trial of the case in which the juror is sitting. If the juror is called so to testify, the opposing party shall be afforded an opportunity to object out of the presence of the jury.

(b) Inquiry into validity of verdict or indictment.

Upon an inquiry into the validity of a verdict or indictment, a juror may not testify as to any matter or statement occurring during the course of the jury's deliberations or to the effect of anything upon that or any other juror's mind or emotions as influencing the juror to assent to or dissent from the verdict or indictment or concerning the juror's mental processes in connection therewith. But a juror may testify about (1) whether extraneous prejudicial information was improperly brought to the jury's attention, (2) whether any outside influence was improperly brought to bear upon any juror, or (3) whether there was a mistake in entering the verdict onto the verdict form. A juror's affidavit or evidence of any statement by the juror may not be received on a matter about which the juror would be precluded from testifying.

The first jury in the *Spector* trials was unable to reach a verdict, and Judge Fidler declared a mistrial. After the trial Juror #9, Ricardo Enriquez, spoke to the media and indicated that the jury had voted 10 to 2 in favor of conviction. Mr. Enriquez voted for conviction. He also indicated that in his opinion, Juror #10 would never have changed his mind from his vote of not guilty.

Question

606-1 If called as a witness in the second *Spector* trial, would Mr. Enriquez have been allowed to testify about the jury deliberations?

Rule 607. Who May Impeach

The credibility of a witness may be attacked by any party, including the party calling the witness.

In the past, if a party called a witness to the stand, he or she "vouched" for the witness. Therefore, that party was unable to impeach that witness. Today, even if a party calls a witness, that party may impeach the witness. This rule is a recognition that a party may need to call an adverse witness to the stand. Marla is on trial for assaulting Peter, a U.S. Postal Service employee. The government must call Robert, Marla's husband, to testify as a witness. Is the government vouching for the testimony of Robert? No. The government is allowed to impeach Robert.

How does one impeach a witness? There are numerous methods of impeachment, such as showing bias, a prior inconsistent statement, showing that the witness had an obstructed view, and showing that the witness has a reputation for lying.

Questions

607-1   May the prosecution ask Stephanie Jennings (one of the women who testified about Mr. Spector's prior gun violence) whether she was paid $1,200 by the *National Enquirer* magazine for her photos? Why would the prosecution do this?

607-2   May the prosecution ask Dr. Michael Baden, an expert witness called by the defense, whether he is married to Linda Kenney-Baden, one of the defense attorneys?

Rule 608. Evidence of Character and Conduct of Witness

(a) Opinion and reputation evidence of character.

The credibility of a witness may be attacked or supported by evidence in the form of opinion or reputation, but subject to these limitations: (1) the evidence may refer only to character for truthfulness or untruthfulness, and (2) evidence of truthful character is admissible only after the character of the witness for truthfulness has been attacked by opinion or reputation evidence or otherwise.

(b) Specific instances of conduct.

Specific instances of the conduct of a witness, for the purpose of attacking or supporting the witness' character for truthfulness, other than conviction of crime as provided in Rule 609, may not be proved by extrinsic evidence. They may, however, in the discretion of the court, if probative of truthfulness or untruthfulness, be inquired into on cross-examination of the witness (1) concerning the witness' character for truthfulness or untruthfulness, or (2) concerning the character for truthfulness or untruthfulness of another witness as to which character the witness being cross-examined has testified.

The giving of testimony, whether by an accused or by any other witness, does not operate as a waiver of the accused's or the witness' privilege against self-incrimination when examined with respect to matters that relate only to character for truthfulness.

A witness is called to the stand at trial. Should that witness be subject to character assassination? This should occur, if at all, only if the questioning relates to a very relevant issue. What is relevant when a witness testifies? Whether his or her testimony is accurate. This rule addresses situations in which the character of the witness may be attacked.

Consider the following: Juan sues the Nuclear Regulatory Commission because he was injured in an accident at a nuclear facility. Sofia testifies on Juan's behalf because she witnessed the accident.

- May the defense ask her whether she cheats on her husband? Of course not — it is irrelevant.
- May the defense ask Sophia if she is dating Juan? Yes, that would show bias.
- May the defense call William, a fellow employee, to testify that Sofia has a reputation for lying? Yes, it is relevant. This is reputation evidence.
- May the defense ask William whether Sophia is known for "sleeping around?" No, it is irrelevant.
- During the cross-examination of William, may Juan's counsel ask him whether Sophia filed a complaint against him two years ago for sexual harassment? Yes, that would show his bias against Sophia. This is a specific instance of conduct.
- If William replies "no" to the question about the sexual harassment complaint, may Juan's counsel introduce the complaint into evidence? Yes. This is extrinsic evidence. Juan's counsel may inquire about the complaint, and may introduce it into evidence. It shows bias.
- During the cross-examination of William, may Juan's counsel ask him whether he lied on a bank application for a loan one year ago? Yes. This is a specific instance of conduct.
- If William replies "no" to the question about the bank loan, may Juan's counsel introduce the application for the bank loan into evidence? No. This is extrinsic evidence. Juan's counsel may inquire about the bank loan, but may not introduce it into evidence. It shows untruthfulness.

In 2003, the Advisory Committee amended Rule 608(b) to clarify a point that had led to a split in the Circuit Courts of Appeal. The rule previously read "specific instances of the conduct of a witness, for the purpose of attacking or supporting the witness' **credibility**, other than conviction of crime as provided in Rule 609, may not be proved by extrinsic evidence." The rule was changed to read as it is now, "specific instances of the conduct of a witness, for the purpose of attacking or supporting the witness' **character for truthfulness**, other than conviction of crime as provided in Rule 609, may not be proved by extrinsic evidence." What is the difference between these two versions, and why was it changed?

The rule was changed because there was a difference of opinion in the Circuit Courts of Appeal about the use of extrinsic evidence for impeachment purposes (the Advisory Committee cited to the American Bar Association Section of Litigation's *Emerging Problems Under the Federal Rules of Evidence*). Some courts found that extrinsic evidence was prohibited only when used in connection with proving a witness's truthfulness. Other courts held that extrinsic evidence was disallowed in every impeachment situation, including when showing bias, a lack of perception, etc. The Advisory Committee amended the rule to provide that extrinsic evidence is only disallowed in the first instance, when used to show untruthfulness. What exactly is extrinsic evidence? It is generally thought of as extraneous evidence or coming from external sources.

The difference between "credibility" and "character for truthfulness" is shown above — in one instance extrinsic evidence is allowed into evidence (the complaint for sexual harassment) and in the other instance it is not (the bank loan). Why the different treatment? It is believed that extrinsic evidence can take a judge or jury off center. We want to avoid a trial within a trial. Did William really lie on his bank application? Did he receive the loan as a result of the lie? Did he pay back the loan? Was he ever arrested for this lie? The jury may be distracted and this information really is not necessary. Therefore, if William indicates that he did not lie on the loan application, Juan's counsel must "accept the answer." See *United States v. Martz*, 964 F.2d 787, 789 (8th Cir. 1992); and *United States v. Zidell*, 323 F.3d 412 (6th Cir. 2003). It is really a collateral issue. It is deemed more important and thus not collateral if the issue is, for example, bias or mental capacity. "By limiting the application of the Rule to proof of a witness' character for truthfulness, the amendment leaves the admissibility of extrinsic evidence offered for other grounds of impeachment (such as contradiction, prior inconsistent statement, bias and mental capacity) to Rules 402 and 403." Advisory Committee Notes to the 2003 Amendment to Rule 608.

Questions

608-1   May the prosecution ask the defense experts how much they charged for their services in connection with the *Spector* case? If one of the defense witnesses answers incorrectly, may the prosecution introduce into evidence a detailed billing statement from the witness?

608-2   May the defense ask Melissa Grosvenor (one of the women who testified about Mr. Spector's prior gun violence) whether she lied on an employment application when asked about her criminal history? If she answers "no," may the defense introduce into evidence the employment application?

608-3   May the defense ask Stephanie Jennings (another woman who testified about Mr. Spector's prior gun violence) whether she continued to date Mr. Spector after the incidents she described? If she denies dating him, may the defense call another witness to describe the continued dating?

608-4   May the defense ask Adriano De Souza how long it had been since he slept when he allegedly heard Mr. Spector state "I think I killed somebody?"

608-5   After Dorothy Melvin (another woman who testified about Mr. Spector's prior gun violence) testified that she "made it a point" of never being alone with Mr. Spector after the gun incident, may the defense call Nicole Spector to testify that Melvin accompanied she and her father on a trip to Toronto, Canada after the incident?

608-6   May the defense ask Adriano De Souza whether he lied on his applications for visa renewal by misstating his status as a student?

608-7   May the defense ask Adriano De Souza if he was in the country illegally on the day of the shooting? May the defense ask him if he negotiated an arrangement with the government to stay in the country if he testified in this case?

Rule 609. Impeachment by Evidence of Conviction of Crime

(a) General rule.

For the purpose of attacking the character for truthfulness of a witness,

   (1) evidence that a witness other than an accused has been convicted of a crime shall be admitted, subject to Rule 403, if the crime was punishable by death or imprisonment in excess of one year under the law under which the witness was convicted, and evidence that an accused has been convicted of such a crime shall be admitted if the court determines that the probative value of admitting this evidence outweighs its prejudicial effect to the accused; and

   (2) evidence that any witness has been convicted of a crime shall be admitted, regardless of the punishment, if it readily can be determined that establishing the elements of the crime required proof or admission of an act of dishonesty or false statement by the witness.

(b) Time limit.

Evidence of a conviction under this rule is not admissible if a period of more than ten years has elapsed since the date of the conviction or of the release of the witness from the confinement imposed for that conviction, whichever is the later date, unless the court determines, in the interests of justice, that the probative value of the conviction supported by specific facts and circumstances substantially outweighs its prejudicial effect. However, evidence of a conviction more than 10 years old as calculated herein, is not admissible unless the proponent gives to the adverse party sufficient advance written notice of intent to use such evidence to provide the adverse party with a fair opportunity to contest the use of such evidence.

(c) Effect of pardon, annulment, or certificate of rehabilitation.

Evidence of a conviction is not admissible under this rule if (1) the conviction has been the subject of a pardon, annulment, certificate of rehabilitation, or other equivalent procedure based on a finding of the rehabilitation of the person convicted, and that person has not been convicted of a subsequent crime that was punishable by death or imprisonment in excess of one year, or (2) the conviction has been the subject of a pardon, annulment, or other equivalent procedure based on a finding of innocence.

(d) Juvenile adjudications.

Evidence of juvenile adjudications is generally not admissible under this rule. The court may, however, in a criminal case allow evidence of a juvenile adjudication of a witness other than the accused if conviction of the offense would be admissible to attack the credibility of an adult and the court is satisfied that admission in evidence is necessary for a fair determination of the issue of guilt or innocence.

(e) Pendency of appeal.

The pendency of an appeal therefrom does not render evidence of a conviction inadmissible. Evidence of the pendency of an appeal is admissible.

Like Rule 608(b), Rule 609 was amended by the Advisory Committee in 2006. The earlier version of the rule read "for the purpose of attacking the **credibility** of a witness . . ." The new version changed the word credibility to **character for truthfulness**. According to the Advisory Committee, "the limitations of Rule 609 are not applicable if a conviction is admitted for a purpose other than to prove the witness's character for truthfulness." The rule is inapplicable, for example if used to show contradiction. See *United States v. Lopez*, 979 F.2d 1024 (5th Cir. 1992).

The rule was amended also to clarify part (a)(2) of the rule — that the crime is only admissible if the conviction **required proof** of an act of dishonesty or false statement. The types of crimes that fall under this section are those such as forgery, perjury, false statement, or fraud, among others. If the witness simply said something untruthful during the commission of the offense, the offense would not be admissible. Therefore, if an individual, during a theft, states she has a gun when in fact she does not have a gun, the crime would not be one that would fall within this part of the rule. Look to the statute or indictment to determine if the offense required proof of an act of dishonesty or false statement.

Questions

609-1   May the defense ask Melissa Grosvenor (one of the witnesses who testified about Mr. Spector's prior gun violence) whether she had ever been convicted of embezzlement?

609-2   In the event Mr. Spector had testified at trial, would the State be allowed to introduce his prior charged offense of assault with a firearm (two felony counts) and brandishing a firearm (two misdemeanor counts)? Mr. Spector pleaded guilty to one count of brandishing a firearm.

Rule 611. Mode and Order of Interrogation and Presentation

(a) Control by court.
  The court shall exercise reasonable control over the mode and order of interrogating witnesses and presenting evidence so as to (1) make the interrogation and presentation effective for the ascertainment of the truth, (2) avoid needless consumption of time, and (3) protect witnesses from harassment or undue embarrassment.

(b) Scope of cross-examination.
  Cross-examination should be limited to the subject matter of the direct examination and matters affecting the credibility of the witness. The court may, in the exercise of discretion, permit inquiry into additional matters as if on direct examination.

(c) Leading questions.
  Leading questions should not be used on the direct examination of a witness except as may be necessary to develop the witness' testimony. Ordinarily leading questions should be permitted on cross-examination. When a party calls a hostile witness, an adverse party, or a witness identified with an adverse party, interrogation may be by leading questions.

Judge Fidler allowed the entertainment/news media to televise the first *Spector* trial. The defense had objected to this action. The following is the text of California Rules of Court, Rule 1.150(e):

(e) *Media coverage*
  Media coverage may be permitted only on written order of the judge as provided in this subdivision. The judge in his or her discretion may permit,

refuse, limit, or terminate media coverage. This rule does not otherwise limit or restrict the right of the media to cover and report court proceedings.

(1) *Request for order*

The media may request an order on **Media Request to Photograph, Record, or Broadcast** (form MC-500). The form must be filed at least five court days before the portion of the proceeding to be covered unless good cause is shown. A completed, proposed order on **Order on Media Request to Permit Coverage** (form MC-510) must be filed with the request. The judge assigned to the proceeding must rule on the request. If no judge has been assigned, the request will be submitted to the judge supervising the calendar department, and thereafter be ruled on by the judge assigned to the proceeding. The clerk must promptly notify the parties that a request has been filed.

(2) *Hearing on request*

The judge may hold a hearing on the request or may rule on the request without a hearing.

(3) *Factors to be considered by the judge*

In ruling on the request, the judge is to consider the following factors:

(A) The importance of maintaining public trust and confidence in the judicial system;

(B) The importance of promoting public access to the judicial system;

(C) The parties' support of or opposition to the request;

(D) The nature of the case;

(E) The privacy rights of all participants in the proceeding, including witnesses, jurors, and victims;

(F) The effect on any minor who is a party, prospective witness, victim, or other participant in the proceeding;

(G) The effect on the parties' ability to select a fair and unbiased jury;

(H) The effect on any ongoing law enforcement activity in the case;

(I) The effect on any unresolved identification issues;

(J) The effect on any subsequent proceedings in the case;

(K) The effect of coverage on the willingness of witnesses to cooperate, including the risk that coverage will engender threats to the health or safety of any witness;

(L) The effect on excluded witnesses who would have access to the televised testimony of prior witnesses;

(M) The scope of the coverage and whether partial coverage might unfairly influence or distract the jury;

(N) The difficulty of jury selection if a mistrial is declared;

(O) The security and dignity of the court;

(P) Undue administrative or financial burden to the court or participants;

(Q) The interference with neighboring courtrooms;

(R) The maintenance of the orderly conduct of the proceeding; and

(S) Any other factor the judge deems relevant.

During the jury deliberation in the first *Spector* trial, the government asked Judge Fidler to instruct the jury on a lesser-included offense, involuntary manslaughter. The judge declined to do so. He did withdraw a "pinpoint" instruction — "special Instruction Number 3" which provided as follows:

> It is the prosecution's contention that the act committed by the defendant that caused the death of Ms. Clarkson was to point a gun at her, which resulted in that gun entering Ms. Clarkson's mouth while in Mr. Spector's hand . . . If you do not find that the prosecution has proved beyond a reasonable doubt that the defendant committed that act, you must return a verdict of not guilty.

The judge had asked the jury if there was anything he could do to help it with its impasse. The jury indicated that Special Instruction Number 3 was causing them some difficulty.

Judge Fidler also allowed the jury to tour Mr. Spector's mansion during the course of the trial, although he did rule that Mr. Spector's wife Rachelle could not be present during the tour. There was also a controversy prior to the visit because the prosecution obtained an email in which Richard Gabriel, a jury consultant for Mr. Spector, wrote "Fountain will be on full bore for site visit tomorrow, yes?" The prosecution maintained that this was meant to convince the jury that Adriano De Souza was unable to hear Mr. Spector adequately when he heard "I think I killed someone." The judge ruled that there was no evidence that the fountain was actually capable of being set low or high.

Mr. Spector's lead counsel for this third trial team (lead counsel for the first trial team was Robert Shapiro; and lead counsel for the second trial team was Leslie Abramson (who achieved fame representing the Menendez brothers)) was Bruce Cutler. Mr. Cutler was reportedly bombastic in his questioning of witnesses and Judge Fidler told him that he needed to question witnesses from the lectern and not threaten them. In one instance, the judge strongly warned Mr. Cutler to change his behavior. See http://www.youtube.com/watch?v=1bOk_TWMQjY.

The judge ruled on July 19, 2007, that Jody "Babydol" Gibson could not discuss Lana Clarkson with the media. Do you agree with the judge's rulings?

Rule 612. Writing Used to Refresh Memory

Except as otherwise provided in criminal proceedings by section 3500 of title 18, United States Code, if a witness uses a writing to refresh memory for the purpose of testifying, either—

(1) while testifying, or
(2) before testifying, if the court in its discretion determines it is necessary in the interests of justice, an adverse party is entitled to have the writing produced at the hearing, to inspect it, to cross-examine the witness thereon, and to introduce in evidence those portions which relate to the testimony of the witness. If it is claimed that the writing contains matters not related to the subject matter of the testimony the court shall examine the writing in camera, excise any portions not so related, and order delivery of the remainder to the party entitled thereto. Any portion withheld over objections shall be preserved and made available to the appellate

court in the event of an appeal. If a writing is not produced or delivered pursuant to order under this rule, the court shall make any order justice requires, except that in criminal cases when the prosecution elects not to comply, the order shall be one striking the testimony or, if the court in its discretion determines that the interests of justice so require, declaring a mistrial.

For writings used during the trial, this is an absolute rule and the judge has no discretion. The rule is worded that the adverse party "is entitled." The judge does have discretion for writings used before testifying.

This rule is referred to as "Refreshing Recollection" — anything may be used to refresh recollection, including inadmissible evidence because the item used to refresh recollection need not ever be entered into evidence. It is merely a memory device — the evidence is the recollection it actually triggers. This rule is often confused with Past Recollection Recorded, a hearsay exception (Rule 803(5)). They are completely different rules, although often used in conjunction with each other. Refreshing recollection is a prerequisite to the use of Past Recollection Recorded. Anything may be used to refresh recollection – a sound, a smell, a physical object, a writing, etc.

Rule 613. Prior Statements of Witnesses

(a) Examining witness concerning prior statement.
   In examining a witness concerning a prior statement made by the witness, whether written or not, the statement need not be shown nor its contents disclosed to the witness at that time, but on request the same shall be shown or disclosed to opposing counsel.
(b) Extrinsic evidence of prior inconsistent statement of witness.
   Extrinsic evidence of a prior inconsistent statement by a witness is not admissible unless the witness is afforded an opportunity to explain or deny the same and the opposite party is afforded an opportunity to interrogate the witness thereon, or the interests of justice otherwise require. This provision does not apply to admissions of a party-opponent as defined in Rule 801(d)(2).

This rule is referred to as "Prior Inconsistent Statements." This rule is often confused with Federal Rule of Evidence 801(d)(1)(A), a rule that deems a statement "not hearsay." The difference between Rule 613 and Rule 801(d)(1)(A) is that Rule 613 statements are often used for impeachment purposes only and are not offered "for the truth of the matter asserted." Prior inconsistent statements were offered by the prosecution to refute the defense allegation that Ms. Clarkson was depressed and shot herself in Mr. Spector's home.

The defense called a number of witnesses who knew Ms. Clarkson and elicited from them their beliefs that Ms. Clarkson was suicidal. Three of the more powerful witnesses were Jennifer Hayes-Riedl, Irene "Punkin' Pie" Laughlin, and Gregory Sims.

Ms. Hayes-Riedl testified that Ms. Clarkson had been one of her very best friends and that she, Lana, and "Punkin' Pie" had been "thick as theives." She testified for the defense at trial that Lana had been "out of her mind depressed." She described Ms. Clarkson as "sad and pathetic." On cross-examination, the prosecutor asked about statements Ms. Hayes-Riedl made to a defense investigator before the trial. She had stated the following (among other things) about Ms. Clarkson:

Every man was a meal ticket to her
She would always have one-night stands
Her family had this "disgusting sexy memorial" service
She was the most selfish person you'd ever meet
She wasn't so cute anymore
She gained weight — on her hips
She would sleep with anyone

Irene "Punkin' Pie" Laughlin testified that she believed Ms. Clarkson was suicidal and that Ms. Clarkson told her twice that she wanted to commit suicide. She said that Ms. Clarkson used the painkiller Vicodin recreationally and was humiliated by her job at the House of Blues. On cross-examination, the prosecution asked her about a letter she had previously written in which she stated the following:

My Lana, my best friend, my right arm, my inseparable sister, was violently and abruptly taken from me at the hands of Phil Spector.

Punkin' Pie further testified that just days before her death, Ms. Clarkson was ignored by Michael Bay (movie director of *Pearl Harbor, Bad Boys, Transformers*) at a party. She said Ms. Clarkson began to cry and said, "I hate this town and I hate the people in it and I don't want to be here anymore."

Greg Sims, an independent film producer, was called by the defense and he testified that Ms. Clarkson was at a party he was throwing at the St. Regis Hotel shortly before her death. He said that she became distraught after the party, and said she did not want to go on. He testified that she was very depressed and was as down as he'd ever seen anyone.

Questions

613-1 May the prosecution ask Ms. Hayes-Riedl why she would say rather uncomplimentary things about her very good friend?

613-2 May the prosecution ask Punkin' Pie whether she said "absolutely not" when asked by police officers after the shooting whether Ms. Clarkson's personality suggested suicide?

613-3 May the prosecution enter into evidence the letter written by Punkin' Pie?

613-4 May the prosecution show the jury an interview clip from CourtTV in which Mr. Sims stated the following:

- that Ms. Clarkson seemed low before her death, but that given her situation that was totally normal
- that "under no circumstances" did she take her own life
- that she would not take out a gun and shoot herself

613-5 May the prosecution call to the stand Lisa Bloom, the interviewer on CourtTV, to testify about the statements made by Mr. Sims?

Rule 615. Exclusion of Witnesses

At the request of a party the court shall order witnesses excluded so that they cannot hear the testimony of other witnesses, and it may make the order of its own motion. This rule does not authorize exclusion of (1) a party who is a natural person, or (2) an officer or employee of a party which is not a natural person designated as its representative by its attorney, or (3) a person whose presence is shown by a party to be essential to the presentation of the party's cause, or (4) a person authorized by statute to be present.

Questions

615-1 Is this rule mandatory, or is the exclusion of witnesses within the judge's discretion?

615-2 May one of the experts testifying on behalf of Mr. Spector be excluded from the courtroom?

ARTICLE VII. OPINIONS AND EXPERT TESTIMONY

Rule 701. Opinion Testimony by Lay Witnesses

If the witness is not testifying as an expert, the witness' testimony in the form of opinions or inferences is limited to those opinions or inferences which are (a) rationally based on the perception of the witness, and (b) helpful to a clear understanding of the witness' testimony or the determination of a fact in issue, and (c) not based on scientific, technical, or other specialized knowledge within the scope of Rule 702.

In the past, a "lay witness" — one who is not testifying as an expert — was not allowed to give opinion testimony. The lay witness was allowed only to testify to "facts." Attempting to differentiate fact from opinion was, in practice, very difficult. If a witness testifies that an attacker was "heavy set" is that a fact or an opinion?

Due to the difficulty in separating fact from opinion, the rule now allows a lay witness to testify to his or her opinions, but only if the opinion is based upon his or her rational perceptions, and the opinion is helpful to the jury's clear understanding of the witness's testimony. Part (c) was added later in order to prohibit a party from making an "end run" around the expert witness rules by simply calling an expert as a lay witness and then have him or her also testify about areas within his or her expertise. The reason a party would want to do this is because there are particular procedural rules (for example, notice requirements) that apply when an expert is involved, and these are not triggered when a lay witness testifies.

What exactly is the difference between what opinion may be offered by a lay witness and an expert? The Advisory Committee cites to *State v. Brown* in its notes and states, "In Brown, the court declared that the distinction between lay and expert witness testimony is that lay testimony "results from a process of reasoning familiar in everyday life," while expert testimony "results from a process of reasoning which can be mastered only by specialists in the field." Advisory Committee Notes to Rule 701, citing to *State v. Brown*, 836 S.W.2d 530, 549 (Tennessee 1992).

In the *Spector* trial, Mr. Spector's high school friend and dinner date the evening of February 2, 2003, Rommie Davis, testified that Mr. Spector "was not his usual self" the evening of the shooting. She said she could not tell whether he was drunk but that she was concerned about him because he was drinking and taking medication and it was a "lethal combination."

Los Angeles Sheriff's Detective Mark Lilienfeld testified that he found a Viagra pill in Mr. Spector's briefcase on the morning of the shooting. He found a container that held one pill and had two empty slots. Detective Lilienfeld stated that he was suspicious that a sex crime had occurred. He based this belief upon the Viagra pill, the "romantic scene" in the living room, lit candles, a nearly empty brandy snifter in the bathroom, false eyelashes in the bathroom, and the way Ms. Clarkson was dressed.

Greg Sims testified that Lana Clarkson was a "close friend" of his. He testified that she was in a "distressed state" the evening he saw her, which was shortly before her death. He was also asked if she was depressed.

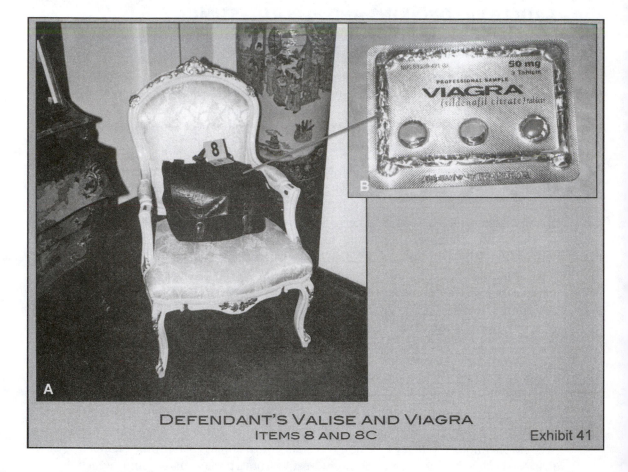

DEFENDANT'S VALISE AND VIAGRA
ITEMS 8 AND 8C

Exhibit 41

Questions

701-1   May Ms. Davis testify as indicated above?
701-2   May Detective Lilienfeld testify about his suspicions?
701-3   May Mr. Sims testify about Ms. Clarkson's mental state?
701-4   Should the Judge allow Adriano De Souza to testify that he smelled alcohol coming from the back of the limo on the evening in question? May Adriano De Souza testify that Mr. Spector "had a stupid look on his face?

Rule 702. Testimony by Experts

If scientific, technical, or other specialized knowledge will assist the trier of fact to understand the evidence or to determine a fact in issue, a witness qualified as an expert by knowledge, skill, experience, training, or education, may testify thereto in the form of an opinion or otherwise, if (1) the testimony is based upon sufficient facts or data, (2) the testimony is the product of reliable principles and methods, and (3) the witness has applied the principles and methods reliably to the facts of the case.

Expert witness testimony was extremely important in the *Spector* trial. Many experts testified, including the following:

For the Prosecution	For the Defense
Dr. John Andrews	Dr. Michael Baden
Dr. Lynne Herold	Dr. Vincent DiMaio
Dr. Lewis Peña	Elizabeth F. Loftus
Steven Renteria	Dr. Robert Alan Middleburg
	Dr. Werner Spitz

The State of California made much of the fact that Mr. Spector spent $419,000 on experts for his trial. The reference to this fact in the prosecution's closing statement is one of Mr. Spector's grounds for appeal.

As the rule indicates, the proponent of expert testimony must show that specialized knowledge will assist the trier of fact (judge or jury) to understand a fact in issue. The expert must be qualified in that his or her knowledge must exceed that of the jury on the issue in question. Qualification may be made by showing education or experience. For example, a cowboy may qualify as an expert even if that individual has no more than an elementary school education. Provided he or she has more knowledge than the jurors (what is the average cost of a bull?), he or she may testify. The subject matter of the testimony must be beyond the knowledge of the average juror.

If the subject matter of the expert testimony is considered "novel," the theory of science, technology, or other specialized knowledge must be reliable. The theory must be applied reliably. According to the Advisory Committee Notes, "there is no more certain test for determining when experts may be used than the common sense inquiry whether the untrained layman would be qualified to determine intelligently and to the best possible degree the particular issue without enlightenment from those having a specialized understanding of the subject involved in the dispute." Advisory Committee Notes to Rule 702, citing to Ladd, *Expert Testimony*, 5 Vand. L. Rev. 414, 418 (1952). Would an expert be necessary to inform the judge that marijuana is a drug? No. This is within the average knowledge of a juror. May an expert testify about the street value of marijuana in 2009? Yes. This is not within the average knowledge of a juror.

If the method used by the expert is considered novel, the method itself must be shown reliable. Suppose an expert has a theory that those who eat broccoli are five times more likely to commit murder. Should this expert be allowed to testify about his or her theory? Only if it is shown that his or her theory is reliable. In the past, the test for whether a method was reliable was whether it had gained *general acceptance* in the particular field in which it belongs. See *Frye v. United States*, 293 F. 1013 (D.C. Cir. 1923). In 1993, the United States Supreme Court rejected the *Frye* test and found that novel scientific evidence need not be generally accepted in order to be admissible. *Daubert v. Merrell Dow Pharmaceuticals*, 509 U.S. 579 (1993). This new approach is referred to as the *"Daubert* Test." The Supreme Court announced that the trial judge should be the "gatekeeper" of this novel evidence and should consider certain factors, such as the following:

1. Whether the expert's technique or theory can be or has been tested
2. Whether the technique or theory has been subject to peer review and publication
3. The known or potential rate of error of the technique or theory when applied
4. The existence and maintenance of standards and controls
5. Whether the technique or theory has been generally accepted in the scientific community (the old *Frye* standard)

These factors are non-exclusive. In *Kumho Tire v. Carmichael*, the Supreme Court decided that the *Daubert* analysis applied to non-scientific novel evidence cases as well (such as technical or other specialized knowledge). 526 U.S. 137 (1999). In *General Electric Co. v. Joiner*, the Court determined that the correct standard of review of a case on appeal is "abuse of discretion." 522 U.S. 136 (1997). In other words, the appellate court should reverse the decision of the trial court judge (the "gatekeeper") only if the trial judge abused his or her discretion in allowing an expert to testify on a novel theory. These three Supreme Court cases (*Daubert, Kumho*, and *Joiner*) are referred to as the "trilogy of cases" on novel expert evidence.

The Advisory Committee lists five additional factors for the judges to consider (but again, not an exhaustive list). These have been taken from the *Kumho* and *Joiner* cases, and are the following:

1. Whether experts are "proposing to testify about matters growing naturally and directly out of research they have conducted independent of the litigation, or whether they have developed their opinions expressly for purposes of testifying"
2. Whether the expert has unjustifiably extrapolated from an accepted premise to an unfounded conclusion
3. Whether the expert has adequately accounted for obvious alternative explanations
4. Whether the expert "is being as careful as he would be in his regular professional work outside his paid litigation consulting"
5. Whether the field of expertise claimed by the expert is known to reach reliable results for the type of opinion the expert would give

Expert witnesses are exempt from the rule that requires personal knowledge (Rule 602). Elizabeth Loftus was allowed to testify about Adriano De Souza's testimony even though she had never met Mr. De Souza. She testified that memories are affected by what happens after the initial event and those who are "confident" in their memories are only slightly more likely to be correct than those who are not.

The defense objected to the testimony of three prosecution witnesses — Dr. Louis Peña, Dr. Lynne Herold, and Steven Renteria. According to the defense, part of Dr. Pea's testimony was beyond the scope of his expertise. He was qualified to testify as to the results of his autopsy, according to the defense, but not about Ms. Clarkson's mental state and whether she was suicidal.

The defense maintained that Dr. Herold's testimony was objectionable because, although she was a member of the International Association of Bloodstain Pattern Analysts, she took only one course on bloodstain analysis before she analyzed the evidence in this case.

Steven Renteria's testimony about "luminol testing" was objectionable according to the defense because it did not meet the "general acceptance" standard followed in California. California follows the *Frye* test and has not adopted the federal *Daubert* test. *People v. Kelly*, 549 P.2d 1240 (Cal. 1976). If you have ever watched an episode of *CSI: Crime Scene Investigation*, you are familiar with luminol. Luminol reacts with hemoglobin in blood and produces a bluish-green light. Investigators spray it at a crime scene to detect the presence of blood. It was sprayed at Mr. Spector's residence the day of the shooting. The State of California answered these objections by arguing that the objection really goes to the weight of the evidence, not its admissibility. The weight was for the jury to decide. In other words, the process met the standard, and the jury was free to believe it or disbelieve it.

The government experts conceded that they found neither Mr. Spector's DNA nor his fingerprints on the gun from which the bullet that killed Ms. Clarkson came. Dr. Vincent DiMaio, who testified for the defense, concluded that Lana Clarkson was "an aging, out-of-work actress fighting depression and health problems." He also testified that the caps on Ms. Clarkson's teeth were blown out of her body by gasses in the mouth, not by the recoil of the gun. The bruising on the tongue was caused by the exploding gasses. According to Dr. DiMaio, Lana Clarkson's system had evidence of alcohol, Vicodin, and Benadryl, which were all "central nervous depressants." He stated, "that's where people get drunk and do stupid things. That's what they do."

Prosecution witness Jamie Lintemoot testified that Ms. Clarkson had blood on the back of her hand. The defense cross-examined her on the use of acetate tape to lift the bloodstains off Ms. Clarkson's dress. Defense expert Dr. Middleberg testified that Ms. Clarkson's blood-alcohol level was likely .12 at the time of the shooting, above the legal limit of .08. He further found that the urine test performed on Mr. Spector did not prove conclusively that he was intoxicated.

Dr. Baden (a defense expert) explained that he had an "aha!" moment on a Sunday during the pendency of the trial. He indicated that Ms. Clarkson's spine was not completely transected immediately and she could have breathed for three or four minutes after she was shot, which would explain the blood spatters on Mr. Spector's jacket that he received when he was rendering aid to her. Judge Fidler accused the defense of a "deliberate and egregious" violation of the discovery rules in order to "gain a tactical advantage and to throw the prosecution off their game." This was due to the fact that the defense had not disclosed

Dr. Baden's new theory to the prosecution. Dr. Andrews was called as a "rebuttal" witness by the prosecution and he stated that Ms. Clarkson would have suffered "spinal shock," which would have prevented any reflex movement of the body.

On December 15, 2008, the People of the State of California filed a Motion to Exclude Evidence of a "Psychological Autopsy." A psychological autopsy is conducted after a death, where evidence is gathered to determine whether someone could have committed suicide.

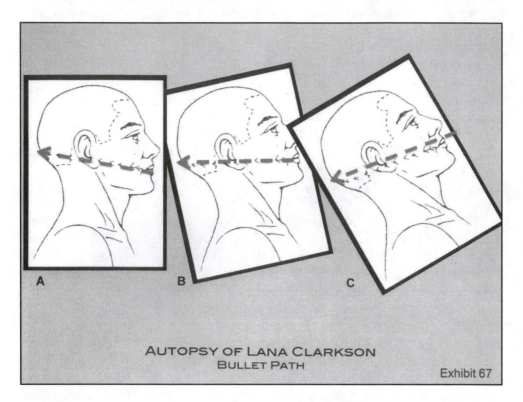

AUTOPSY OF LANA CLARKSON
BULLET PATH

Exhibit 67

Questions

702-1 Should Dr. Peña be allowed to testify concerning Ms. Clarkson's mental state?

702-2 Is Dr. Herold's testimony admissible?

702-3 Would luminol testing be allowable under the *Daubert* test?

702-4 Should Dr. DiMaio be allowed to testify as indicated above?

702-5 What would you want to know to determine whether the "psychological autopsy" is admissible in evidence?

Rule 703. Bases of Opinion Testimony by Experts

The facts or data in the particular case upon which an expert bases an opinion or inference may be those perceived by or made known to the expert at or before the

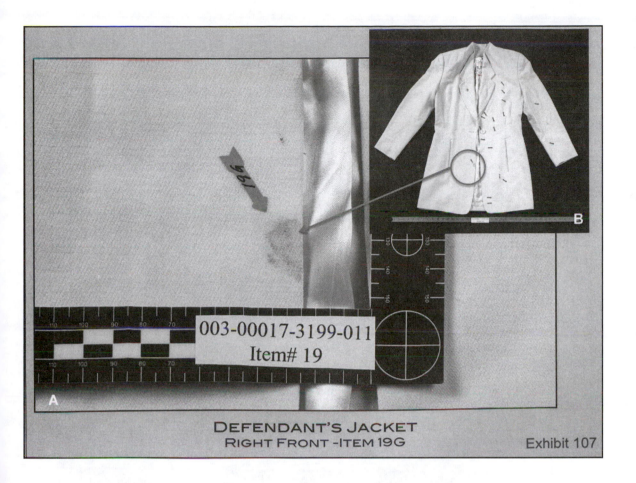

DEFENDANT'S JACKET
RIGHT FRONT -ITEM 19G

Exhibit 107

hearing. If of a type reasonably relied upon by experts in the particular field in forming opinions or inferences upon the subject, the facts or data need not be admissible in evidence in order for the opinion or inference to be admitted. Facts or data that are otherwise inadmissible shall not be disclosed to the jury by the proponent of the opinion or inference unless the court determines that their probative value in assisting the jury to evaluate the expert's opinion substantially outweighs their prejudicial effect.

Note that an expert may rely on otherwise inadmissible evidence — provided it is the type of information normally relied upon by experts in the field. For example, an expert may testify based on hearsay statements made to him or her, if the statements are of the type relied on by experts in that field.

According to the defense, Dr. Peña's testimony was objectionable because he relied on information obtained from sources *after* he performed the autopsy.

Question

703-1 Is Dr. Peña's testimony allowed under this rule?

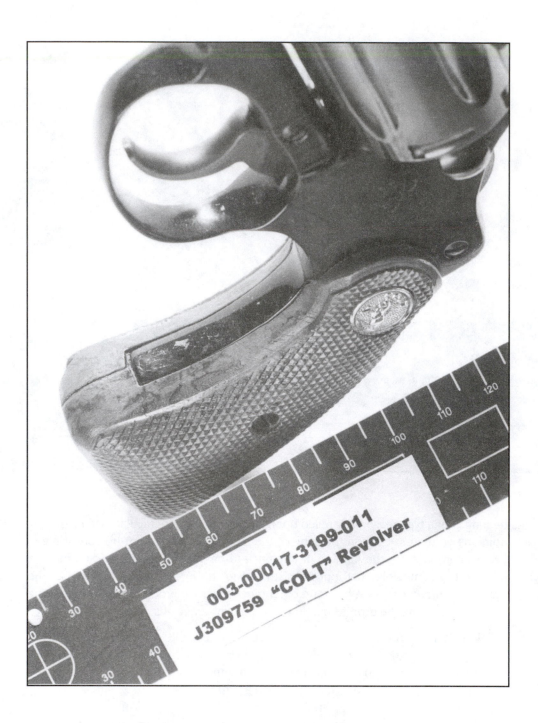

Rule 704. Opinion on Ultimate Issue

(a) Except as provided in subdivision (b), testimony in the form of an opinion or inference otherwise admissible is not objectionable because it embraces an ultimate issue to be decided by the trier of fact.

(b) No expert witness testifying with respect to the mental state or condition of a defendant in a criminal case may state an opinion or inference as to whether the defendant did or did not have the mental state or condition constituting an element of the crime charged or of a defense thereto. Such ultimate issues are matters for the trier of fact alone.

Dr. Vincent DiMaio testified for the defense that in his opinion Lana Clarkson was suicidal and she killed herself. Dr. Werner Spitz unequivocally concluded that the gunshot wound was self-inflicted.

Question

704-1 Are Doctors DiMaio's and Spitz's opinions admissible under this rule?

ARTICLE VIII. HEARSAY

Rule 801. Definitions

The following definitions apply under this article:

(a) Statement.
A "statement" is (1) an oral or written assertion or (2) nonverbal conduct of a person, if it is intended by the person as an assertion.

(b) Declarant.
A "declarant" is a person who makes a statement.

(c) Hearsay.
"Hearsay" is a statement, other than one made by the declarant while testifying at the trial or hearing, offered in evidence to prove the truth of the matter asserted.

(d) Statements which are not hearsay.
A statement is not hearsay if —

(1) *Prior statement by witness.* The declarant testifies at the trial or hearing and is subject to cross-examination concerning the statement, and the statement is (A) inconsistent with the declarant's testimony, and was given under oath subject to the penalty of perjury at a trial, hearing, or other proceeding, or in a deposition, or (B) consistent with the declarant's testimony and is offered to rebut an express or implied charge against the declarant of recent fabrication or improper influence or motive, or (C) one of identification of a person made after perceiving the person; or

(2) *Admission by party-opponent.* The statement is offered against a party and is

(A) the party's own statement, in either an individual or a representative capacity or

(B) a statement of which the party has manifested an adoption or belief in its truth, or

(C) a statement by a person authorized by the party to make a statement concerning the subject, or

(D) a statement by the party's agent or servant concerning a matter within the scope of the agency or employment, made during the existence of the relationship, or

(E) a statement by a coconspirator of a party during the course and in furtherance of the conspiracy.

The contents of the statement shall be considered but are not alone sufficient to establish the declarant's authority under subdivision (C), the agency or employment relationship and scope thereof under subdivision (D), or the existence of the conspiracy and the participation therein of the declarant and the party against whom the statement is offered under subdivision (E).

Hearsay is one of the most important of the Federal Rules of Evidence. It applies to all "statements" offered into evidence. A statement is virtually anything said outside of the courtroom, or anything written. What makes the rule particularly challenging is the large number of exceptions to the rule. Generally, hearsay is defined as an *out of court statement used to prove the truth of the matter asserted*. Hearsay is not allowed at the trial unless it is either defined as "not hearsay," or fits into one of the many exceptions in the Rules. The reason that hearsay is not allowed is that it is considered unreliable and untrustworthy. Why? Because the statement was made outside of court, and there was no opportunity to cross-examine the speaker. Hearsay also implicates the "Confrontation Clause" from the Sixth Amendment to the United States Constitution. A defendant in a criminal case has the right to confront his or her accusers against him or her. See below.

Hearsay is excluded when it is offered "for the truth of the matter asserted." But what does that mean? A simple way of looking at this is to ask whether the statement is being offered to show that the *statement itself* is true. If the statement is being offered to show something else, then it is not hearsay.

For example: Ethel wrote a will in 1999 in which she gave all of her property to her son Phillip. She later changed her will to completely exclude Phillip. Phillip challenges the will, and claims that Ethel did not have the mental capacity to write the second will. He offers the testimony of Martin, who plans to state that for two months prior to her death, Ethel consistently told him that she was the Queen of England. Are the statements hearsay? They are "out of court" statements — they were said by Ethel outside of the courtroom (she is now dead). But, are they being offered to actually prove Ethel is in fact the Queen of England? No. They are being offered to show that Ethel thought she was the Queen of England and thus lacked the mental capacity to execute a will. The statements are not hearsay.

Sometimes hearsay can occur without any words being spoken. Suppose the prosecution wishes to call a police officer to testify that when she arrived at the scene of a crime and asked who committed the crime, someone pointed to the defendant. No words were spoken. Is there any hearsay? Yes. The definition of hearsay includes nonverbal conduct if meant as an assertion. The action of pointing was meant as an assertion, and is hearsay in this instance. Silence may also be a statement, if ordinarily a person would speak under the circumstances. *Rahn v. Hawkins*, 464 F.3d 813, 821 (8th Cir. 2006). If a police officer arrived at the scene of a crime and asked an individual "did you do it?" most individuals would respond under those circumstances.

There are several types of statements that are defined as "not hearsay." First, if a statement is not being offered for the truth of the matter asserted, it is not hearsay. Other statements that are not hearsay include: some "prior statements by witness" and an "admission by party-opponent." A prior statement by a witness is actually a fairly narrow category. These are only statements where the declarant testifies at the trial and is subject to cross examination, **and** the prior statement was given under oath. The statement in question must be 1) inconsistent with the current testimony; or 2) consistent with the current testimony, but presented to rebut an express or implied charge of fabrication; or 3) a statement of identification.

An admission of a party-opponent is defined as "not hearsay." In this situation a statement is offered against the party who actually made the statement. It is not hearsay because the person should not be able to complain about no prior opportunity to cross-examine himself/herself. Additionally, there is no confrontation clause issue because he or she would only be confronting himself/herself.

Five different categories of statements fall within an admission of a party-opponent: the party's own statement; a statement that the party has adopted as their own; a statement made by a person authorized to make the statement on behalf of the party; a statement made by an agent of the party, concerning a matter within the scope of the agency or employment, made during the existence of the relationship; and anything said by a co-conspirator (even if the party joined the conspiracy after the statement was made, and even if there is no formal charge of conspiracy).

For example: Wang is accused of burglary. When questioned by the police prior to the trial, Wang said he was at a restaurant at the time of the burglary. During the trial, he claims that he was at home at the time of the burglary. His earlier statement is an "admission of a party opponent" if offered by the prosecution. It is not an admission of a party opponent if offered by him because he is not his own party opponent.

Undoubtedly the most important piece of evidence at the trial was Adriano De Souza's testimony of what Mr. Spector said to him the morning of the shooting. According to Mr. DeSouza, Mr. Spector said "I think I killed somebody." The defense maintained that Mr. De Souza did not correctly hear Mr. Spector because he was too far away, he had just woken up, the water fountain was running (which was located between Mr. De Souza and the door of the castle), and because English was his second language.

The State called Vincent Tannazzo to testify about statements made by Mr. Spector in 1993 and 1994 at celebrity Joan Rivers's holiday parties. Mr. Tannazzo was a retired New York City police detective hired as security for the party. The defense objected strenuously to his testimony. Tannazzo testified that, when being escorted out of the party, Mr. Spector stated "I ought to put a bullet in her (expletive) head right now." He also indicated that Mr. Spector was "ranting" and used an obscenity to describe women. Tannazzo indicated that Mr. Spector also said "they all deserve a bullet in their heads."

Questions

801-1 May Mr. De Souza testify about Mr. Spector's statement the morning of the shooting?

801-2 May the State introduce the tape recording of statements made by Mr. Spector after he was shot with a Taser gun and before he was arrested?

801-3 Are Mr. Spector's statements at the police station admissible?

801-4 Mr. Spector spoke to the media (*Esquire* magazine) after the evening of the shooting (the interview was in July of 2003). He stated the following: "She kissed the gun. I have no idea why—I never knew her, never even saw her before that night. I have no idea who she was or what her agenda was . . . There is no case . . . She killed herself. She was loud and drunk even before we left the club. She grabbed a bottle of tequila to take with her." Are these statements admissible by the defense?

801-5 Should Vincent Tannazzo's testimony be admissible? What about under Rule 403?

Rule 802. Hearsay Rule

Hearsay is not admissible except as provided by these rules or by other rules prescribed by the Supreme Court pursuant to statutory authority or by Act of Congress.

Question

802-1 May Mr. De Souza testify that Lana said to him as she entered the limo that she was "going just for a drink" and that Mr. Spector replied to her "Don't talk to the driver!"?

Confrontation Clause

Text of the Confrontation Clause to the Sixth Amendment to the United States Constitution:

> [i]n all criminal prosecutions, the accused shall enjoy the right . . . to be confronted with the witnesses against him.

It must be emphasized that the Clause refers to "the accused." The Confrontation Clause applies only to criminal cases. For approximately 24 years, the Confrontation Clause was virtually indistinguishable from the hearsay rules. Compare *Ohio v. Roberts*, 448 U.S. 56 (1980) with *Crawford v. Washington*, 541 U.S. 36 (2004). In 2004, the slumbering giant that was the confrontation clause came back to life in a big way in *Crawford v. Washington*.

In *Crawford*, Michael Crawford was accused of the assault and attempted murder of Kenneth Lee. Michael asserted that he stabbed Lee in self-defense. At trial, Michael's wife Sylvia did not testify because of the spousal testimonial privilege. The government introduced Sylvia's earlier tape-recorded statement to the police in which she stated that she saw nothing in Lee's hand at the time of the stabbing. Michael objected to the use of the police interrogation statement as a violation of his right to confrontation. The Washington State Supreme Court determined that the statement did not violate his right to confrontation under the old *Ohio v. Roberts* test that was in effect at the time. That test provided that the use of an unavailable witness's statement did not violate a defendant's right to confrontation as long as the statement bore "adequate indicia of reliability." 448 U.S. 56, 66 (1980). In order to bear adequate indicia of reliability, the statement had to either fall within a "firmly rooted hearsay exception," or "bear particularized guarantees of trustworthiness." Generally this meant that the confrontation clause analysis and the hearsay analysis were one and the same — as all of the hearsay exceptions were adopted because the statements were in some way considered trustworthy. Michael's attorney argued that the analysis had strayed from the original meaning of the confrontation clause. The Supreme Court agreed, and we now have a new test (or rather, tests) for the Confrontation Clause.

Justice Scalia, who delivered the majority opinion, went far back into history to decipher the meaning of the Confrontation Clause. He found that cross-examination was the key. The government should not be able to introduce certain statements into evidence unless the defendant had a prior opportunity to cross-examine his or her accuser. Only certain statements, however. Only those statements deemed "**testimonial**," which he defined as "ex parte in-court testimony or its **functional equivalent**."

Therefore, the definition of "testimonial" is crucial. The Supreme Court did not define testimonial in *Crawford*, except to say that it applies "at a minimum to prior testimony at a preliminary hearing, before a grand jury, at a former trial, and to police 'interrogations.'"

One question that arose after the *Crawford* case is what exactly is police "interrogation"? Some answers were provided in the *Davis v. Washington*, 547 U.S. 813 (2006) case. In that case, the question was whether a 911 emergency call to the police was considered "testimonial." The Supreme Court differentiated between a 911 call in which the **primary purpose** is to enable police to respond to an "ongoing emergency" versus a call with the primary purpose to establish or prove past events potentially relevant to later criminal prosecution. To the extent the call is simply to allow the police to respond to an ongoing emergency, the call is nontestimonial and there is no Confrontation Clause issue. If on the other hand the call is to establish events with an eye toward later prosecution, the call is testimonial.

If an expert relies on "testimonial" statements in reaching his or her opinion, and testifies at trial, the Confrontation Clause is not triggered. See *United States v. Johnson*, 587 F.3d 625 (4th Cir. 2009). In *Giles v. California*, the Supreme Court clarified the "forfeiture by wrongdoing" doctrine of the Confrontation Clause. In order for a defendant to forfeit his or her right to confrontation, he or she must make the witness unavailable **for the purposes of testifying**. *Giles v. California*, 554 U.S. — , 128 S. Ct. 2678 (2008). It is not enough that the defendant made the witness unavailable — the defendant must do this with the specific intent to prevent the witness from testifying. Therefore if Aleksei murders his ex-wife Elena because he is furious about the divorce, he has not waived the confrontation clause by wrongdoing.

Questions

6th A-1 Would Mr. Spector's blood-alcohol and toxicology reports be admissible under the Confrontation Clause in the absence of the scientist who prepared the reports? If not, must the State present both the nurse who supervised the giving of the urine sample, and the scientist who analyzed the urine?

COUNTY OF LOS ANGELES

DEPARTMENT OF CORONER
1104 N. MISSION RD., LOS ANGELES, CALIFORNIA 90033
Forensic Science Laboratories
March 04, 2003

nthony T. Hernandez
rector

L. Sathyavagiswaran, M.D.
Chief Medical Examiner-Coroner

Sergeant Steve Katz
Los Angles County Sheriff's Department-Homicide
5747 Rickenbacker Road
Commerce, CA 90040

RE: Los Angeles County Department of Coroner Lab No. 2003-OC-02
       LASD DR No. 003-00017-3199-011   Spector, Phillip
       LASD Evidence Receipt No. J321678

On February 06, 2003 the laboratory received a sealed manila envelope containing a sealed "Step 9" white envelope with a 50-ml capacity, purple plastic capped centrifuge tube labeled "Spector, Phillip 2-3-03 1700 BD 12-26-39" with approximately 9-10 ml of urine.

It was requested that our laboratory perform a general toxicology screen as well as specific tests for Motrin® (Ibuprofen), Seroquel® (Quetiapine), Amitriptyline, Diphenhydramine, Hydrocodone, Zyprexa® (Olanzapine), Topamax® (Topiramate), Prozac® (Fluoxetine), and Loxapine. The following is a report of those analyses:

Results-Drugs	Specimen	Method	Concentration
Barbiturates	Urine	ELISA	Not Detected
Cocaine, Cocaethylene, & Benzoylecgonine	Urine	GC/MS	Not Detected
Fentanyl	Urine	ELISA	Not Detected
Methamphetamine	Urine	ELISA	Not Detected
Opiates (Codeine, Morphine & Hydrocodone)	Urine	ELISA	Not Detected
Phencyclidine (PCP)	Urine	ELISA	Not Detected
Ethanol	Urine	GC/FID Headspace	0.07 g%
Acid/Neutral Drug Screen			
Topiramate	Urine	GC/MS	37 ug/ml
Ibuprofen	Urine	GC/MS	Not Detected
Pharmaceutical or Basic Drug Screen			
Fluoxetine	Urine	GC/NPD & GC/MS	0.46 ug/ml
Norfluoxetine	Urine	GC/NPD & GC/MS	0.23 ug/ml
Diphenhydramine	Urine	GC/NPD & GC/MS	Not Detected
Amitriptyline	Urine	GC/NPD & GC/MS	Not Detected
Nortriptyline	Urine	GC/NPD & GC/MS	Not Detected
Loxapine	Urine	GC/NPD & GC/MS	Not Detected
Amoxapine	Urine	GC/NPD & GC/MS	Not Detected
Olanzapine	Urine	GC/NPD & GC/MS	Not Detected
Quetiapine	Urine	GC/NPD & GC/MS	Not Detected

The specimen is being returned to the custody of the Los Angeles Sheriff's Department.

Dan Anderson
Supervising Criminalist II
Toxicology Laboratory

002090

0201

6th A-2   Is Mr. Spector's Confrontation Clause right implicated if he (Mr. Spector) is able to call the government scientist as a witness but chooses not to do so?

6th A-3   Imagine a situation where Ms. Clarkson had an earlier altercation with Mr. Spector and that she provided information to the police about the earlier incident. Would Mr. Spector have forfeited his right of confrontation?

6th A-4   On appeal, Mr. Spector argues that showing a videotape of prior hearing testimony (at the Caplan hearing) upon which Judge Fidler comments violates the Confrontation Clause. Do you agree?

COUNTY OF LOS ANGELES - SHERIFF'S DEPARTMENT
SCIENTIFIC SERVICES BUREAU
LABORATORY REPORT

BLOOD ALCOHOL TESTING SECTION		File Number:	003-00017-3199-011
7717 Golondrinas Street		Agency:	LASD Homicide
Downey, CA 90242		Investigator:	Katz (323) 890-5581
(562) 940-0328		Charge:	187 P.C.
		Report Date:	July 2, 2003

Subject: Spector, Phil

Victim: Clarkson, Lana

This is a supplemental report to that issued by the undersigned on April 3, 2003.

On March 31, 2003, Detective Katz provided a hypothetical drinking pattern including the following information:

One male weighing 135 pounds was drinking alcohol from approximately 10:00 p.m. until approximately 2:30 a.m. The alcohol was consumed in the following manner, with times indicated based on bar bills:

    10:17 p.m.:   (2) daiquiris at "The Grill", each daiquiri containing approximately 1 shot of rum.
    10:41 p.m. to 12 a.m.: (2) Navy Grogs at "Trader Vics", each containing approximately 3 shots of rum.
    1:27 a.m.:   (2) daiquiris at "Dan Tana's"
    1:59 a.m. to 2:30 a.m.: (1) shot of 151 at "House of Blues".

The drinks described would contain approximately six ounces of pure alcohol (100% v/v).

I was asked by Detective Katz to estimate what this person's blood alcohol level might be at approximately 5 a.m.

CONCLUSIONS:

Based on the hypothetical, the above described male could potentially reach a blood alcohol level of approximately .19% at 5 a.m.

This is just an approximation based on information provided. If the information were different, different estimations could be obtained. It is also possible, based on other physiological factors not addressed, that this person could have a blood alcohol level lower than a .19% at 5 a.m.

Examination by: Catherine L. Navetta,

                  Senior Criminalist

007507

Rule 803. Hearsay Exceptions; Availability of Declarant Immaterial

The following are not excluded by the hearsay rule, even though the declarant is available as a witness:

(1) Present sense impression. A statement describing or explaining an event or condition made while the declarant was perceiving the event or condition, or immediately thereafter.

(2) Excited utterance. A statement relating to a startling event or condition made while the declarant was under the stress of excitement caused by the event or condition.

(3) Then existing mental, emotional, or physical condition. A statement of the declarant's then existing state of mind, emotion, sensation, or physical condition (such as intent, plan, motive, design, mental feeling, pain, and bodily health), but not including a statement of memory or belief to prove the fact remembered or believed unless it relates to the execution, revocation, identification, or terms of declarant's will.

(4) Statements for purposes of medical diagnosis or treatment. Statements made for purposes of medical diagnosis or treatment and describing medical history, or past or present symptoms, pain, or sensations, or the inception or general character of the cause or external source thereof insofar as reasonably pertinent to diagnosis or treatment.

(5) Recorded recollection. A memorandum or record concerning a matter about which a witness once had knowledge but now has insufficient recollection to enable the witness to testify fully and accurately, shown to have been made or adopted by the witness when the matter was fresh in the witness' memory and to reflect that knowledge correctly. If admitted, the memorandum or record may be read into evidence but may not itself be received as an exhibit unless offered by an adverse party.

(6) Records of regularly conducted activity. A memorandum, report, record, or data compilation, in any form, of acts, events, conditions, opinions, or diagnoses, made at or near the time by, or from information transmitted by, a person with knowledge, if kept in the course of a regularly conducted business activity, and if it was the regular practice of that business activity to make the memorandum, report, record or data compilation, all as shown by the testimony of the custodian or other qualified witness, or by certification that complies with Rule 902(11), Rule 902(12), or a statute permitting certification, unless the source of information or the method or circumstances of preparation indicate lack of trustworthiness. The term "business" as used in this paragraph includes business, institution, association, profession, occupation, and calling of every kind, whether or not conducted for profit.

(7) Absence of entry in records kept in accordance with the provisions of paragraph (6). Evidence that a matter is not included in the memoranda reports, records, or data compilations, in any form, kept in accordance with the provisions of paragraph (6), to prove the nonoccurrence or nonexistence of the matter, if the matter was of a kind of which a memorandum, report, record, or data compilation was regularly made and preserved, unless the sources of information or other circumstances indicate lack of trustworthiness.

(8) Public records and reports. Records, reports, statements, or data compilations, in any form, of public offices or agencies, setting forth (A) the activities of the office or agency, or (B) matters observed pursuant to duty imposed by law as to which matters there was a duty to report, excluding, however, in criminal cases matters observed by police officers and other law enforcement personnel, or (C) in civil actions and proceedings and against the Government in criminal cases, factual findings resulting from an investigation made pursuant to authority granted by law, unless the sources of information or other circumstances indicate lack of trustworthiness.

(9) Records of vital statistics. Records or data compilations, in any form, of births, fetal deaths, deaths, or marriages, if the report thereof was made to a public office pursuant to requirements of law.

(10) Absence of public record or entry. To prove the absence of a record, report, statement, or data compilation, in any form, or the nonoccurrence or nonexistence of a matter of which a record, report, statement, or data compilation, in any form, was regularly made and preserved by a public office or agency, evidence in the form of a certification in accordance with Rule 902, or testimony, that diligent search failed to disclose the record, report, statement, or data compilation, or entry.

(11) Records of religious organizations. Statements of births, marriages, divorces, deaths, legitimacy, ancestry, relationship by blood or marriage, or other similar facts of personal or family history, contained in a regularly kept record of a religious organization.

(12) Marriage, baptismal, and similar certificates. Statements of fact contained in a certificate that the maker performed a marriage or other ceremony or administered a sacrament, made by a clergyman, public official, or other person authorized by the rules or practices of a religious organization or by law to perform the act certified, and purporting to have been issued at the time of the act or within a reasonable time thereafter.

(13) Family records. Statements of fact concerning personal or family history contained in family Bibles, genealogies, charts, engravings on rings, inscriptions on family portraits, engravings on urns, crypts, or tombstones, or the like.

(14) Records of documents affecting an interest in property. The record of a document purporting to establish or affect an interest in property, as proof of the content of the original recorded document and its execution and delivery by each person by whom it purports to have been executed, if the record is a record of a public office and an applicable statute authorizes the recording of documents of that kind in that office.

(15) Statements in documents affecting an interest in property. A statement contained in a document purporting to establish or affect an interest in property if the matter stated was relevant to the purpose of the document, unless dealings with the property since the document was made have been inconsistent with the truth of the statement or the purport of the document.

(16) Statements in ancient documents. Statements in a document in existence twenty years or more the authenticity of which is established.

(17) Market reports, commercial publications. Market quotations, tabulations, lists, directories, or other published compilations, generally used and relied upon by the public or by persons in particular occupations.

(18) Learned treatises. To the extent called to the attention of an expert witness upon cross-examination or relied upon by the expert witness in direct examination, statements contained in published treatises, periodicals, or pamphlets on a subject of history, medicine, or other science or art, established as a reliable authority by the testimony or admission of the witness or by other expert testimony or by judicial notice. If admitted, the statements may be read into evidence but may not be received as exhibits.

(19) Reputation concerning personal or family history. Reputation among members of a person's family by blood, adoption, or marriage, or among a person's associates,

or in the community, concerning a person's birth, adoption, marriage, divorce, death, legitimacy, relationship by blood, adoption, or marriage, ancestry, or other similar fact of personal or family history.

(20) Reputation concerning boundaries or general history. Reputation in a community, arising before the controversy, as to boundaries of or customs affecting lands in the community, and reputation as to events of general history important to the community or State or nation in which located.

(21) Reputation as to character. Reputation of a person's character among associates or in the community.

(22) Judgment of previous conviction. Evidence of a final judgment, entered after a trial or upon a plea of guilty (but not upon a plea of nolo contendere), adjudging a person guilty of a crime punishable by death or imprisonment in excess of one year, to prove any fact essential to sustain the judgment, but not including, when offered by the Government in a criminal prosecution for purposes other than impeachment, judgments against persons other than the accused. The pendency of an appeal may be shown but does not affect admissibility.

(23) Judgment as to personal, family or general history, or boundaries. Judgments as proof of matters of personal, family or general history, or boundaries, essential to the judgment, if the same would be provable by evidence of reputation.

(24) [Other exceptions.] [Transferred to Rule 807]

When one first views Rules 803, 804, and 807, one may wonder why we have a hearsay rule at all. It appears that the exceptions swallow the rule. In actual practice, many statements are excluded by the hearsay rule. Why all the exceptions? Many of these exceptions were developed over hundreds of years by case law. Each one of the exceptions exists because the statement in issue is considered reliable and trustworthy. "The present rule proceeds upon the theory that under appropriate circumstances, a hearsay statement may possess circumstantial guarantees of trustworthiness sufficient to justify nonproduction of the declarant in person at the trial even though he may be available." Advisory Committee Note to Rule 803. The Rule 803 exceptions apply regardless of whether the declarant is available, whereas the 804 exceptions apply only in the event the party shows the declarant is "unavailable."

Remember that the declarant is the person who made the statement, who is not necessarily the person testifying. In the example below, George is the declarant. George, Frank, or anyone else who heard the statement may be called to testify to the content of the statement.

The first exception under Rule 803 is "present sense impression." There are three requirements under this rule: the statement must describe and explain the event; the declarant must have in fact seen the event; and the statement must be made at the time, or very close to the time of the event. The time requirement is especially important. Generally, the statement must be made within just a few seconds of witnessing the event.

For example: George and Frank are walking down the street. As they are walking, they see Henry ride by on his bicycle. Henry is talking on his cell phone while he is riding. George says to Frank, "There goes Henry — talking on his cell phone while he is riding — that's dangerous." The statement that George made would fall under present sense impression because it was made at the time George saw Henry and it describes what George saw.

The next exception is called "excited utterance." In this case there must be a startling event and the declarant must still be under the stress of the event when the statement is made. There is no time period requirement as there is for present sense impression, but the declarant must be under the stress of the situation, and obviously that stress likely will wane over time.

For example: Mary runs to her neighbor Elaine's house and screams "oh my gosh, my husband just hit me with a pipe! I think he's trying to kill me."

A "then existing mental, emotional, or physical condition" is another exception under Rule 803. A statement is not hearsay if it describes "the declarant's **then existing** state of mind, emotion, sensation, or physical condition (such as intent, plan, motive, design, mental feeling, pain and bodily health)."

For example: Jin tells Nikolai, "I am terrified of Mark — he's a maniac." This is a "then existing" mental condition. If Jin says "Mark scared the heck out of me last night" it is not a "then existing" state of mind. Generally, statements concerning events in the future may be admissible, for example, "I expect to leave Wichita on or about March the 5th with a certain Mr. Hillmon . . . " *Mutual Life Ins. Co. v. Hillmon*, 145 U.S. 285 (1892). Statements concerning past events are not admissible, for example "Dr. Shepard has poisoned me." *Shepard v. U.S.*, 90 U.S. 96 (1933).

Statements made for the purposes of medical diagnosis or treatment are another exception. The statements a patient makes to a doctor or other health care professional are excluded from the hearsay rule if they are "made for medical diagnosis or treatment and describing medical history, or past or present symptoms, pain, or sensations, or the inception or general character of the cause or external source." However, the statements *must be related* to the treatment or diagnosis. The theory behind this exception is that since a person is going to the doctor for treatment, that person would be unlikely to tell the doctor false information, because his or her health depends upon telling the truth. Statements about causation are generally not allowed.

For example: Arianna tells the nurse when she arrives at the emergency room that she has pain in her lower leg. This statement would fall into an exception to the hearsay rule. If she also states "it's because this idiot in a blue car ran over me," that statement would not fall within the exception.

"Recorded recollection" is excluded from the hearsay rule under Rule 803(5). This is commonly referred to as "past recollection recorded." A recorded recollection is a statement about something that a witness once had knowledge of. Procedurally, several steps must be taken before the document is used as a recorded recollection. First, the witness must fail to recollect the details of what he or she earlier wrote or recorded. The memorandum or recording can then be used to refresh the witness's memory (recall the earlier discussion of refreshing recollection under Rule 612). If the witness still is unable to remember, then the recording may be *read* into evidence. The actual memorandum or recording is never admitted into evidence under the exception.

For example: A police officer responds to the scene of a crime and goes directly back to his department and writes a report of his findings. He is later called to testify at trial, but he is unable to remember the exact details of the crime. The party must first attempt to refresh recollection under Rule 612. If that attempt is unsuccessful, the report may be read into evidence, but the actual report is never admitted under Rule 803(5).

The next exception is for "records of regularly conducted activity." This exception is known as the *business records exception*. Rule 803(6) excludes from the hearsay rule memorandums, reports, records, or data compilations made during the normal course of business. The rule has many procedural requirements that must be met prior to admission. The rationale for the rule is due to the need of businesses to keep reliable records. "Business" includes non-profit organizations and associations and organizations of any kind.

For example: Tyler's Tire Store keeps records of every tire sale. Included in these records are: the name of the person who purchased the tire; what type of tire the person purchased; how many tires were purchased; how much was paid for the tire; and the date the tire was purchased. The employee who sells the tires fills out the report at the time the tires are purchased. There is a caveat in the rule — "unless the source of information or the method or circumstances of preparation indicate a lack of trustworthiness." If an individual slipped on water in a grocery store, and an employee subsequently prepared an accident report, the report may not be completely trustworthy.

The last major exception under Rule 803 is "public records," Rule 803(8). This exception is similar to the business records exception, however this exception is for public (governmental) agencies. The rule allows into evidence records that are either internal documents, matters observed pursuant to an employee's duty to report, or factual findings resulting from an investigation. However, matters observed by police officers or other law enforcement personnel are not excluded from the hearsay rule in criminal cases. The reason for this exclusion is that the officer is preparing his report in preparation for the criminal case. Those reports are not considered trustworthy enough to fall within the exception under the hearsay rule. As a society, we want the officer to actually appear and testify at trial.

In the *Spector* case, the defense offered into evidence messages that Lana Clarkson sent by email to her friends. The following are some of the statements contained in the emails:

- I have been and will need your funds to get through this long cold winter ahead! I have applied for a personal loan from my SF investor. It will be the last one I can get from him. If he does that is . . . If not, Bye Bye cottage, hello street!
- Over here things are pretty bad. I won't go into detail, but I am on the verge of losing it all. Just hanging on by a thread.
- I am truly at the end of his whole deal. I am going to tidy my affairs and chuck it, 'cuz it's really all too much for just this girl to bear anymore.

LOS ANGELES COUNTY DISTRICT ATTORNEY'S OFFICE

In the Matter of:)
)
People of the   )
State of California,   )
)
                          Plaintiff,   )
)
)
          v.   )
) Case No. GA048824
Phillip Spector,   )
)
                          Defendant.   )
_____)

TRANSCRIPTION OF TAPE-RECORDED 911 CALL BY

ADRIANO DE SOUZA ON FEBRUARY 3, 2003

1

COUNTY OF LOS ANGELES DISTRICT ATTORNEY'S OFFICE

1

2

3

4   In the Matter of:) Case No. GA048824
)
5   Transcription of taped 911 Call   )
     On February 3, 2003.   )
6   _____   )

7

8

9

10

11

12

13   Transcription of tape-recorded 911 Call BY

14   Adriano DeSouza to the CALIFORNIA HIGHWAY

15   PATROL and the ALHAMBRA POLICE DEPARTMENT

16   on February 3, 2003.

17

18

19   CLERK: C.H.P. Certification Clerk

20   CHP: C.H.P. Operator

21   ALHAMBRA: Alhambra P.D. Operator

22   DE SOUZA: Adriano De Souza

23   OFFICER: Unidentified Alhambra Police Officer

24   ***: Unintelligible
25

                          2

```
 1            COUNTY OF LOS ANGELES; FEBRUARY 3, 2003

 2                          --o0o--

 3

 4        CLERK:  California Highway Patrol, Los Angeles

 5   Communications Center, for February 3, 2003.  All 9-1-1

 6   calls related to log number 235, 1700 Grandview Drive in

 7   Alhambra are included.  This tape runs from approximately

 8   05:00 to 05:10 hours.  Long blank spaces and/or

 9   transmissions not concerning this incident have been

10   deleted.  This tape was prepared on December 29, 2003, at

11   08:01 hours by Public Safety Dispatch Supervisor I Sandra

12   Hill, I.D. Number Adam-9316.

13        I hereby certify that this cassette recording is a

14   true copy of the original master tape on file with

15   Department of the California Highway Patrol, Los Angeles

16   Communications Center, Los Angeles, California.

17        CHP:  9-1-1.  What are you reporting?

18        DE SOUZA:  Hi.  It's a -- my name is Adriano.  I'm,

19   uh, Phil, Phil Spector driver.  I think my boss killed

20   somebody.  Please can, can you send the, uh, uh, a car --

21        CHP:  You think your boss killed somebody?

22        DE SOUZA:  Yes, sir.  Yeah --

23        CHP:  Wha-, what --
```

not personal knowledge

3

COUNTY OF LOS ANGELES DISTRICT ATTORNEY'S OFFICE

1   DE SOUZA: Because I'm a driver. I'm waiting outside

2   and -- I don't know what, what he's -- please send, send,

3   send a --

4   CHP: Okay. Where are you at?

5   DE SOUZA: It's 1700 Grandview Drive. Please.

6   CHP: 1700 Grandview?

7   DE SOUZA: Yes.

8   CHP: And why do you believe he may have killed

9   somebody?

10   DE SOUZA: Because you -- he, he have a lady on the,

11   on the floor and he have a gun in, in his hand.

12   CHP: Okay. Stay on the line. Do not hang up.

13   DE SOUZA: Okay.

14   CHP: You're in Glendale?

15   DE SOUZA: No. I'm in the -- Alhambra. It's

16   1700 Grandview Drive.

17   CHP: Did you hear him shoot or anything?

18   DE SOUZA: Yeah. I hear the, uh, uh, uh, uh -- like a

19   noise. And then he opened the door and "I think he -- I

20   killed her." And then I, I'm, I'm outside the -- the

21   castle --

22   CHP: Okay. Stay on the line.

23   DE SOUZA: Okay.

4

COUNTY OF LOS ANGELES DISTRICT ATTORNEY'S OFFICE

1	CHP: Do not hang up.
2	*[Dial Tone/Telephone Ringing]*
3	ALHAMBRA: Alhambra police.
4	CHP: Alhambra, C.H.P. You got a transfer from an
5	address of 1700 Grandview Drive --
6	ALHAMBRA: Uh-huh.
7	CHP: -- reporting that he thinks his boss just shot
8	and killed a woman.
9	ALHAMBRA: Who? Okay, ***.
10	CHP: He heard the shot, and he says there's a woman
11	laying on the floor and his boss told him he thinks he
12	killed her.
13	ALHAMBRA: Okay. And he's inside the house?
14	CHP: It's inside of a business.
15	ALHAMBRA: Business?
16	CHP: Yeah. I'll bring him online. He's calling from
17	cell phone 310-488-5548.
18	ALHAMBRA: Okay. Hello?
19	CHP: He's on.
20	ALHAMBRA: Sir?
21	DE SOUZA: Yeah.
22	ALHAMBRA: Okay. What happened?
23	DE SOUZA: Oh, my God. Again?

5

COUNTY OF LOS ANGELES DISTRICT ATTORNEY'S OFFICE

```
1        ALHAMBRA:  Oh, okay.  So your boss shot someone?

2        DE SOUZA:  Yeah, I think so.  Because he --

3        ALHAMBRA:  Okay.  You heard a shot?

4        DE SOUZA:  Yeah, I heard the shot outside.  Then I'm

5   outside the castle because I don't know what, what's he

6   gonna --

7        ALHAMBRA:  Is this a business or a residence?

8        DE SOUZA:  No.  It's a residence.

9        ALHAMBRA:  Okay.  So have you seen your boss?

10       DE SOUZA:  Yes.  He had, he had the gun in his hand.

11       ALHAMBRA:  Oh.  Where's the man now?

12       DE SOUZA:  Yeah.  It's a man.

13       ALHAMBRA:  Sir, where's the man?  The man with the

14   gun, where is he?

15       DE SOUZA:  Oh, inside the castle because I'm outside.

16   I'm afraid to go inside again.

17       ALHAMBRA:  But you saw him with the gun?

18       DE SOUZA:  Yeah, I saw him with the gun.

19       ALHAMBRA:  Who did he shoot?

20       DE SOUZA:  I don't know.  I don't know the lady.

21       ALHAMBRA:  Okay, sir.  Stay on the line, okay?

22       DE SOUZA:  Okay.

23       ALHAMBRA:  We're *** someone.
```

6

COUNTY OF LOS ANGELES DISTRICT ATTORNEY'S OFFICE

```
1              DE SOUZA:  Please.  Fast.

2              ALHAMBRA:  Okay.  Hold on, okay?  Sir, is --

3              DE SOUZA:  Yes.

4              ALHAMBRA:  Um, um, you say that that's his -- that's

5       your boss, okay --

6              DE SOUZA:  Yes.

7              ALHAMBRA:  -- do you guys work together?

8              DE SOUZA:  I, I'm, I'm his driver.

9              ALHAMBRA:  Oh, you're his driver?

10             DE SOUZA:  Yeah, I am his driver.

11             ALHAMBRA:  What do you drive?  A taxi or what?

12             DE SOUZA:  I'm dri- -- sorry?

13             ALHAMBRA:  I'm sorry.  What are you driving?

14             DE SOUZA:  I'm driving a Mercedes.

15             ALHAMBRA:  So where are you driving him to?

16             DE SOUZA:  Oh, my God.  Look now --

17             ALHAMBRA:  *** on the way.

18             DE SOUZA:  Okay.

19             ALHAMBRA:  Okay.  So you're his tran- -- his transport

20       service?

21             DE SOUZA:  No.  I'm, I'm a private driver.

22             ALHAMBRA:  Okay.  And your name, sir?

23             DE SOUZA:  Adriano.
```

7

COUNTY OF LOS ANGELES DISTRICT ATTORNEY'S OFFICE

1	ALHAMBRA:	Okay. And your boss' name?
2	DE SOUZA:	It's, uh, Phil Spector.
3	ALHAMBRA:	I'm sorry?
4	DE SOUZA:	Phil Spector.
5	ALHAMBRA:	"Seal?"
6	DE SOUZA:	Spector.
7	ALHAMBRA:	"Seal Inspector?"
8	DE SOUZA:	Yeah. Phil Spector.
9	ALHAMBRA:	That's his name?
10	DE SOUZA:	Yes.
11	ALHAMBRA:	S-e-a-l?
12	DE SOUZA:	P-h-i-l.
13	ALHAMBRA:	C-h- --
14	DE SOUZA:	Spector.
15	ALHAMBRA:	-- i-l. Is he Asian or White or --
16	DE SOUZA:	Sorry?
17	ALHAMBRA:	Is he male White or Asian? Is he an Asian
18		person, a Hispanic person, or a White person?
19	DE SOUZA:	No, it's a White person.
20	ALHAMBRA:	And his name is "Chil" -- C-h-i-l?
21	DE SOUZA:	Yeah. P-h-i-l.
22	ALHAMBRA:	Oh, Phil.
23	DE SOUZA:	Phil, yeah.

8

COUNTY OF LOS ANGELES DISTRICT ATTORNEY'S OFFICE

```
1        ALHAMBRA:   Phil Spector?   Okay.

2        DE SOUZA:   Yes.

3        ALHAMBRA:   Okay.  Do you hear or see him anymore or --

4        DE SOUZA:   Sorry?

5        ALHAMBRA:   Do you see or hear anything else?

6        DE SOUZA:   No.  I'm outside the castle.

7        ALHAMBRA:   Okay.

8        DE SOUZA:   I'm not inside anymore.  I'm afraid to go

9    inside.

10        ALHAMBRA:   I don't want you to, okay?  And what's your

11   name, sir?

12        DE SOUZA:   Oh, I saw the, the, the, the car.

13        ALHAMBRA:   You're inside the car?

14        DE SOUZA:   It's coming.  Yeah.  The police car is

15   coming.

16        ALHAMBRA:   Okay.  Sir, what's your name?

17        DE SOUZA:   Adriano.

18        ALHAMBRA:   Oh, okay.  I'm sorry you gave me that.  And

19   your last name?

20        DE SOUZA:   Souza.  S-o-u-z-a.

21        ALHAMBRA:   Okay.  And your phone number is 310-488-

22   5548?

23        DE SOUZA:   Yes.
```

9

COUNTY OF LOS ANGELES DISTRICT ATTORNEY'S OFFICE

```
 1          ALHAMBRA:   Okay.  Have the units made contact with
 2    you?
 3          DE SOUZA:   Who?
 4          ALHAMBRA:   You say you saw the police near?
 5          DE SOUZA:   No.  He's coming now.
 6          ALHAMBRA:   Okay.
 7          DE SOUZA:   Can I hang up this phone now?
 8          ALHAMBRA:   Okay, hold on.  No.  No.  What color is
 9    your Mercedes?
10          DE SOUZA:   It's black.
11          ALHAMBRA:   I want to make sure that the officer makes
12    contact with you first before I hang up --
13          DE SOUZA:   Okay.
14          DE SOUZA:   He's inside the castle, sir.
15          OFFICER:  Who is?
16          DE SOUZA:   Inside up --
17          OFFICER:  Who is?
18          ALHAMBRA:   Okay, sir, go ahead and talk to him, okay?
19                          [End of Tape]
20
21                          --o0o--
22
23
                              10
```

The prosecution played the De Souza 911 tape to the jury.

The prosecution introduced into evidence the bills from the evening before and the morning of the shooting. The bills were from The Grill, Trader Vic's, Dan Tana's, and House of Blues.

Questions

803-1 Is the tape of the 911 call hearsay? Is it admissible as an exception to the hearsay rule?

803-2 Are the Lana Clarkson emails hearsay? Do they fall within an exception to the hearsay rule?

803-3 Are the restaurant/bar bills hearsay? Do they fall within an exception to the hearsay rule?

803-4 Is the following police report admissible under Rule 803(6)? Is it admissible under Rule 803(8)?

803-5 Would the record of conviction of Mr. Spector in the criminal trial be admissible under Rule 803 in the civil case brought by Lana's mother?

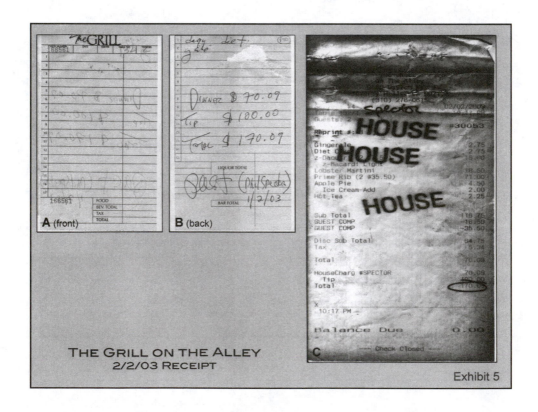

Exhibit 5

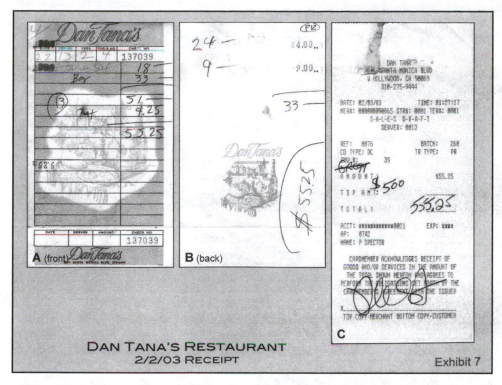

DAN TANA'S RESTAURANT
2/2/03 RECEIPT

Exhibit 7

Rule 804. Hearsay Exceptions; Declarant Unavailable

(a) Definition of unavailability.

"Unavailability as a witness" includes situations in which the declarant —

(1) is exempted by ruling of the court on the ground of privilege from testifying concerning the subject matter of the declarant's statement; or

(2) persists in refusing to testify concerning the subject matter of the declarant's statement despite an order of the court to do so; or

(3) testifies to a lack of memory of the subject matter of the declarant's statement; or

(4) is unable to be present or to testify at the hearing because of death or then existing physical or mental illness or infirmity; or

(5) is absent from the hearing and the proponent of a statement has been unable to procure the declarant's attendance (or in the case of a hearsay exception under subdivision (b)(2), (3), or (4), the declarant's attendance or testimony) by process or other reasonable means.

A declarant is not unavailable as a witness if exemption, refusal, claim of lack of memory, inability, or absence is due to the procurement or wrongdoing of the proponent of a statement for the purpose of preventing the witness from attending or testifying.

(b) Hearsay exceptions.

The following are not excluded by the hearsay rule if the declarant is unavailable as a witness:

(1) *Former testimony.* Testimony given as a witness at another hearing of the same or a different proceeding, or in a deposition taken in compliance with

ALHAMBRA POLICE DEPARTMENT
211 SOUTH FIRST STREET ALHAMBRA, CA 91801
SUPPLEMENTAL REPORT

DR
03-873

DATE	TIME
02/03/03	0502

PARTIES	NAME (LAST,FIRST,MIDDLE)	CODE	ADDRESS	PHONE
	SPECTOR, PHIL	S	1700 GRANDVIEW DR. AIH CA 91803	UNKNOWN
	DE SOUZA, ADRIANO	R		8
	—	—		

CODES: V - VICTIM S - SUSPECT W - WITNESS R - REPORTING PARTY O - OTHER

NARRATIVE

RECEIVED R/C TO RESPOND TO LISTED ADDRESS REGARDING POSSIBLE SHOTS FIRED. UPON ARRIVAL, I CONTACTED R-DESOUZA, WHO IDENTIFIED HIMSELF AS THE DRIVER TO S-SPECTOR. R-DESOUZA STATED S-SPECTOR HAD A GUN AND THAT HE HAD SHOT A WOMAN INSIDE THE RESIDENCE, HE SAID HE SAW HER BODY ON THE FLOOR AND BLOOD ON HER HEAD. HE SAID HE DEFINITELY HEARD WHAT HE THOUGHT TO BE ONE GUN SHOT AND S-SPECTOR SAY TO HIM, "I THINK I KILLED HER."

MYSELF, CORP. PAGE, OFFICERS CARDELLA, HAMMOND AND TAMAYO FORMED AN ENTRY TEAM AND ENTERED THE PROPERTY. WE ENTERED THE N/E DRIVEWAY AND TOOK IT ALL THE WAY TO ITS END. WE OBSERVED WHAT WE DETERMINED TO BE THE BACK DOOR TO THE RESIDENCE. WE FIRST CLEARED A BURGANDY 4-DOOR SEDAN AND THEN ATTEMPTED TO CLEAR THE S/W GARAGE. OFC. CARDELLA STOOD BY THE DOOR TO THE GARAGE FACING NORTH TO KEEP A VISUAL ON THE RESIDENCE. OFC. TAMAYO TOOK A POSITION ON THE S/E CORNER OF THE RESIDENCE ITSELF. WHILE MYSELF, CORP. PAGE AND OFC. HAMMOND COMPLETED OUR CHECK OF THE GARAGE, OFC. CARDELLA ALERTED US, VIA THE RADIO, THAT HE OBSERVED MOVEMENT ON THE SECOND STORY OF THE RESIDENCE. SOON AFTER, OFC. CARDELLA HAD COMPLETE OBSERVATION OF S-SPECTOR VIA THE SOUTH BALCONY. WE ALL FOUR THEN GATHERED AT THE GARAGE DOOR FACING NORTH.

S-SPECTOR SUDDENLY APPEARED IN THE SOUTH DOORWAY TO THE REAR OF THE RESIDENCE. OFC. CARDELLA BEGAN TO GIVE S-SPECTOR VERBAL COMMANDS. OFC. CARDELLA THEN DIRECTED S-SPECTOR TO REMOVE HIS HANDS FROM HIS POCKETS. S-SPECTOR REMAINED STILL AND QUIET. HE THEN WENT BACK INSIDE THE RESIDENCE. AGAIN, OFC. CARDELLA DIRECTED S-SPECTOR TO EXIT THE DOORWAY WITH HIS HANDS IN THE AIR. S-SPECTOR APPEARED BACK IN THE DOORWAY, HOWEVER HE WAS NOT COOPERATIVE IN THAT HE CONTINUED TO IGNORE THE VERBAL COMMANDS GIVEN TO HIM. S-SPECTOR AGAIN WENT BACK INSIDE THE RESIDENCE.

REPORTING OFFICER	PSN	SUPERVISOR APPROVING REPORT	PSN
R. RODRIGUEZ	202	HB/M	

APD FORM REV 9/95en

COPY **SUPPLEMENTAL REPORT**

000025

ALHAMBRA POLICE DEPARTMENT
SUPPLEMENTAL REPORT NARRATIVE

DR 03-873
DATE 02/03/03   PAGE 2 of 3

1 DUE TO THE SEVERITY OF THE SITUATION AND OUR NEED TO CHECK ON
2 ANY INJURED PERSONS INSIDE THE RESIDENCE, WE FOLLOWED S-SPECTOR
3 INTO THE RESIDENCE. S-SPECTOR THEN TURNED TO FACE US. AT THAT
4 TIME, CORP. PAGE TASED S-SPECTOR TO DISABLE HIM AFTER ALL
5 VERBAL COMMANDS HAD FAILED. S-SPECTOR CONTINUED STANDING AS IF
6 THE TASER HAD NO EFFECT ON HIM. OFFICER CARDELLA THEN RUSHED
7 S-SPECTOR USING THE SHIELD TO STRIKE HIM AND KNOCK HIM OFF HIS FEET.
8 OFC. HAMMOND THEN CUFFED S-SPECTOR TO SECURE HIM WHILE WE
9 CONTINUED TO SEARCH THE RESIDENCE.
10
11 UPON ENTERING THE FOYER, I OBSERVED ONE FEMALE ADULT TO MY
12 RIGHT. SHE APPEARED TO BE SITTING ON A CHAIR FACING FORWARD.
13 SHE WAS LIGHT COMPLECTED WITH BLOND HAIR AND WAS BLEEDING
14 ON THE RIGHT SIDE OF HER HEAD. OFC. CARDELLA CHECKED HER FOR
15 ANY SIGNS OF LIFE. HE STATED SHE HAD NO PULSE AND WAS COLD TO
16 HIS TOUCH. THERE WAS A SMALL REVOLVER NEAR HER LEFT FOOT
17
18 I THEN PROCEEDED TO CLEAR THE LOWER LEVEL OF THE WEST WING
19 OF THE RESIDENCE. AS I PROCEEDED TO DO SO, I HEARD S-SPECTOR
20 YELLING "WHAT'S WRONG WITH YOU GUYS?" "WHAT ARE YOU DOING?"
21 AS I CONTINUED WITH MY SEARCH, AGAIN I HEARD S-SPECTOR
22 YELL, "I DIDN'T MEAN TO SHOOT HER, IT WAS AN ACCIDENT." "I HAVE
23 AN EXPLANATION FOR THIS." OFC. CARDELLA THEN JOINED ME AND WE
24 COMPLETED OUR SEARCH OF THE LOWER LEVEL OF THE WEST WING.
25
26 AS OTHER UNITS ARRIVED TO ASSIST, OFC. CARDELLA, MYSELF AND
27 CORP. PAGE THEN PROCEEDED TO THE UPPER LEVEL VIA THE STAIRWAY
28 TO CONTINUE OUR SEARCH. WHEN WE REACHED THE TOP OF THE
29 STAIRWAY, WE WORKED OUR WAY FROM WEST TO EAST CONDUCTING
30 A SYSTEMATIC SEARCH FROM ROOM TO ROOM. ONCE WE DETERMINED
31 THE UPPER LEVEL TO BE SECURE, WE RETURNED TO THE LOWER
32 TO CONTINUE OUR INVESTIGATION.
33
34 AT THAT TIME, TEAM #7 WAS ON SCENE ALONG WITH A.P.D.

REPORTING OFFICER   PSN   SUPERVISOR APPROVING REPORT   PSN
B. RODRIGUEZ   202   116/94   **SUPPLEMENTAL REPORT NARRATIVE**
APD FORM 05, REV 7/91

(20)

000026

ALHAMBRA POLICE DEPARTMENT
REPORT NARRATIVE

DR 03-873
DATE 02/03/03 PAGE 3 OF 3

1 DETECTIVES, WHO ASSUMED CONTROL OF THE CRIME SCENE.

3 A MAJOR INCIDENT LOG WAS GENERATED BY OFC. REYES AND MEDICS
4 RESPONDED TO THE LOCATION AND CONFIRMED THE FEMALE WAS IN FACT
5 DECEASED.

REPORTING OFFICER	PSN	SUPERVISOR APPROVING REPORT	PSN	REPORT NARRATIVE
B RODRIGUEZ	202	16/191		

APD FORM 03, REV 7/91

㉑

000027

law in the course of the same or another proceeding, if the party against whom the testimony is now offered, or, in a civil action or proceeding, a predecessor in interest, had an opportunity and similar motive to develop the testimony by direct, cross, or redirect examination.

(2) *Statement under belief of impending death.* In a prosecution for homicide or in a civil action or proceeding, a statement made by a declarant while believing that the declarant's death was imminent, concerning the cause or circumstances of what the declarant believed to be impending death.

(3) *Statement against interest.* A statement which was at the time of its making so far contrary to the declarant's pecuniary or proprietary interest, or so far tended to subject the declarant to civil or criminal liability, or to render invalid a claim by the declarant against another, that a reasonable person in the declarant's position would not have made the statement unless believing it to be true. A statement tending to expose the declarant to criminal liability and offered to exculpate the accused is not admissible unless corroborating circumstances clearly indicate the trustworthiness of the statement.

(4) *Statement of personal or family history.* (A) A statement concerning the declarant's own birth, adoption, marriage, divorce, legitimacy, relationship by blood, adoption, or marriage, ancestry, or other similar fact of personal or family history, even though declarant had no means of acquiring personal knowledge of the matter stated; or (B) a statement concerning the foregoing matters, and death also, of another person, if the declarant was related to the other by blood, adoption, or marriage or was so intimately associated with the other's family as to be likely to have accurate information concerning the matter declared.

(5) [Other exceptions.][Transferred to Rule 807]

(6) Forfeiture by wrongdoing. A statement offered against a party that has engaged or acquiesced in wrongdoing that was intended to, and did, procure the unavailability of the declarant as a witness.

The Rule 804 exceptions, the other large list of exceptions to the hearsay rule, apply only if the declarant is "unavailable" at trial. Unavailable is defined broadly and includes for example those who claim an evidentiary privilege against testifying, such as the spousal privilege. Each of these once again is allowed in evidence because the statement is considered more trustworthy for some reason than other types of hearsay. For example, former testimony is allowed because the party against whom it is offered had a *prior* opportunity to cross-examine the witness (obviously this type of statement passes muster under the Confrontation Clause as well). The dying declaration is allowed because it is believed that a person would never utter an untruth if he or she believed he or she was about to die (about to meet his or her "maker," as the cases hold). The "forfeiture by wrongdoing" exception is a fairly recent change. It applies if a party was complicit in arranging the "unavailability" of a declarant. This would apply if a defendant killed a witness to a crime. The prior statement of the witness would be allowed into evidence under the hearsay rule (however, there may still be a Confrontation Clause issue). The forfeiture provision under this rule is more relaxed than the forfeiture provision under the Confrontation Clause.

After the first trial and before the second trial, Dianne Ogden died. Ogden was one of the women who testified that Mr. Spector threatened her with a gun.

Questions

804-1 Would the testimony Dianne Ogden gave in the prior *Spector* trial be admissible under this exception to the hearsay rule?

804-2 If Lana Clarkson lived for a short time and Adriano De Souza came to her aid, would statements made by her be admissible under the hearsay rule?

804-3 If Mr. Spector had testified at his trial, would his deposition testimony taken in the *Spector v. Shapiro* case be admissible? Would statements made in the deposition be potentially "statements against interest?" Would you need to use these hearsay exceptions?

Rule 805. Hearsay Within Hearsay

Hearsay included within hearsay is not excluded under the hearsay rule if each part of the combined statements conforms with an exception to the hearsay rule provided in these rules.

Many times a statement may contain hearsay within it. For example, a newspaper article is a perfect example. If Paul Krugman of the *New York Times* writes an article about economics and interviews economist Edward C. Prescott in the article, would that newspaper article be admissible under the hearsay rule? Who is the declarant? Does it make any difference whether Mr. Krugman is present and testifies at trial? The proponent of the evidence must satisfy the hearsay rule for every statement within a statement.

Questions

805-1 Is Officer Rodriguez's report hearsay within hearsay?

805-2 Officer Tannazzo testified at trial that at Joan Rivers's Christmas party, Dorothy Melvin told him that Mr. Spector pulled out a gun at the party. Would this be hearsay? Would this be hearsay within hearsay?

Rule 807. Residual Exception

A statement not specifically covered by Rule 803 or 804 but having equivalent circumstantial guarantees of trustworthiness, is not excluded by the hearsay rule, if the court determines that (A) the statement is offered as evidence of a material fact; (B) the statement is more probative on the point for which it is offered than any other evidence which the proponent can procure through reasonable efforts; and (C) the general purposes of these rules and the interests of justice will best be served by admission of the statement into evidence. However, a statement may not be admitted under this exception unless the proponent of it makes known to the adverse party sufficiently in advance of the trial or hearing to provide the adverse party with a fair opportunity to prepare to meet it, the proponent's intention to offer the statement and the particulars of it, including the name and address of the declarant.

This Rule is sometimes referred to as the "dump rule." If all else fails this exception may be used. Two things to keep in mind — first, the statement must have "circumstantial guarantees of trustworthiness" and the proponent of the evidence must give notice "sufficiently in advance of the trial or hearing."

Question

807-1   If a police report is not admissible under Rule 803(8), might it be admissible under this rule?

ARTICLE IX. AUTHENTICATION AND IDENTIFICATION

Rule 901. Requirement of Authentication or Identification

(a) General provision.

The requirement of authentication or identification as a condition precedent to admissibility is satisfied by evidence sufficient to support a finding that the matter in question is what its proponent claims.

(b) Illustrations.

By way of illustration only, and not by way of limitation, the following are examples of authentication or identification conforming with the requirements of this rule:

(1) *Testimony of witness with knowledge.* Testimony that a matter is what it is claimed to be.

(2) *Nonexpert opinion on handwriting.* Nonexpert opinion as to the genuineness of handwriting, based upon familiarity not acquired for purposes of the litigation.

(3) *Comparison by trier or expert witness.* Comparison by the trier of fact or by expert witnesses with specimens which have been authenticated.

(4) *Distinctive characteristics and the like.* Appearance, contents, substance, internal patterns, or other distinctive characteristics, taken in conjunction with circumstances.

(5) *Voice identification.* Identification of a voice, whether heard firsthand or through mechanical or electronic transmission or recording, by opinion based upon hearing the voice at any time under circumstances connecting it with the alleged speaker.

(6) *Telephone conversations.* Telephone conversations, by evidence that a call was made to the number assigned at the time by the telephone company to a particular person or business, if (A) in the case of a person, circumstances, including self-identification, show the person answering to be the one called, or (B) in the case of a business, the call was made to a place of business and the conversation related to business reasonably transacted over the telephone.

(7) *Public records or reports.* Evidence that a writing authorized by law to be recorded or filed and in fact recorded or filed in a public office, or a purported public record, report, statement, or data compilation, in any form, is from the public office where items of this nature are kept.

(8) *Ancient documents or data compilation.* Evidence that a document or data compilation, in any form, (A) is in such condition as to create no suspicion concerning its authenticity, (B) was in a place where it, if authentic, would likely be, and (C) has been in existence 20 years or more at the time it is offered.

(9) *Process or system.* Evidence describing a process or system used to produce a result and showing that the process or system produces an accurate result.

(10) *Methods provided by statute or rule.* Any method of authentication or identification provided by Act of Congress or by other rules prescribed by the Supreme Court pursuant to statutory authority.

One of the most shocking things to a new practicing lawyer is that a lawyer may not simply give an exhibit to the judge or the jury. How does the document actually make its way to the factfinder (the judge or jury, depending on the circumstances)? If a party wants to introduce bank records into evidence, how does he or she do it? The process is called "laying the foundation." The party must call a foundational witness (unless the parties have entered into a stipulation about the evidence, or unless the evidence is "self-authenticating") in order to move the document into evidence. In this example, a party would need to call the custodian of records at the bank, ask the custodian about the document, elicit testimony that the document is authentic, and then move to have the document admitted, provided the document is admissible under the other evidence rules. Authentication is a prerequisite to admissibility. If a party establishes that an exhibit is authentic, it does not mean the exhibit is admissible. It is merely one of the hurdles toward admissibility.

Authenticating evidence is time consuming and costly — one needs to pay the banker for his or her time, of course. Fortunately, the rules have been relaxed in recent years (see the rules under Rule 902). Although there has been a steady relaxation of the rules, we have problems today that surely no one could have anticipated. Voices may be altered, documents could be easily changed. The process of authentication is showing that an item is what it purports to be. For example, a party must prove that a phone bill really is the phone bill of the person in issue and that it has not been altered in any way.

Consider the revolver, live rounds, and shell casings. How would the State introduce into evidence the revolver found at the scene of the crime and that the live rounds and shell casings came from that revolver? Do we trust that the Los Angeles Sheriff's Department 1) did not make an inadvertent error in handling the evidence, or 2) purposely falsified the evidence? One of the methods of authenticating the evidence in such a case is showing the "chain-of-custody." The State must produce the individual who collected the gun and casings at the scene of the crime, any individuals who transported the gun and casings, the scientist who accepted the gun and casings for testing, the individual who was in charge of the evidence locker, and the person who transported the gun to the courthouse on the day of the trial.

The list in Rule 901 is nonexclusive. It is merely a guide. There may be other methods of authentication.

Questions

901-1 How would you authenticate the tape recording of Mr. Spector that was recorded when he was arrested?

901-2 The defense maintained that the gun was moved during the altercation with Mr. Spector in which he was shot with a Taser gun. How would you authenticate the photograph below?

901-3 How would the Adriano De Souza 911 tape be authenticated?

901-4 How would the defense authenticate emails it maintained were written by Ms. Clarkson?

901-5   It was alleged that Mr. Spector made threatening and obscene phone calls to a couple of the woman mentioned above under "prior bad acts." How would the tape recordings of the phone calls be authenticated?

Rule 902. Self-authentication

Extrinsic evidence of authenticity as a condition precedent to admissibility is not required with respect to the following:

(1)   Domestic public documents under seal. A document bearing a seal purporting to be that of the United States, or of any State, district, Commonwealth, territory, or insular possession thereof, or the Panama Canal Zone, or the Trust Territory of the Pacific Islands, or of a political subdivision, department, officer, or agency thereof, and a signature purporting to be an attestation or execution.

(2)   Domestic public documents not under seal. A document purporting to bear the signature in the official capacity of an officer or employee of any entity included in paragraph (1) hereof, having no seal, if a public officer having a seal and having official duties in the district or political subdivision of the officer or employee certifies under seal that the signer has the official capacity and that the signature is genuine.

(3)   Foreign public documents. A document purporting to be executed or attested in an official capacity by a person authorized by the laws of a foreign country to make the execution or attestation, and accompanied by a final certification as to the genuineness of the signature and official position (A) of the executing or

LOS ANGELES COUNTY SHERIFF'S DEPARTMENT
SCIENTIFIC SERVICES BUREAU
Chemical Processing Section
2020 W. Beverly Boulevard
Los Angeles, CA 90057-2404
voice (213) 989-2171   fax (213) 413-7017

CHEMICAL PROCESSING
EXAMINATION REPORT

AGENCY:	L.A.S.D./Homicide	**FILE NUMBER:**	003-00017-3199-011
INVESTIGATOR:	Det. Fornier	**LAB RECEIPT(S):**	J309759
CHARGE:	187 P.C./Murder	**DATE RECEIVED:**	February 5, 2003
VICTIM(S):	Clarkson, Lana	**SUBJECT(S):**	Spector, Phillip

EVIDENCE SUBMITTED: One white cardboard box, taped and sealed, containing: (1) black "Cobra" revolver with a wooden grip, unknown serial number, .38 special; (5) live rounds in separate manilla envelope; and (1) shell casing removed from the barrel.

RESULTS:

The item(s) were processed for latent prints. No latent prints were developed from the above listed evidence.

DISPOSITION OF EVIDENCE:

All evidence was returned to the Evidence Control Section of the Scientific Services Bureau on June 5, 2003 pending return to the submitting agency, or further examination by another section.

By: FIS II Donna Brandelli, #401547   Date: 6/5/03
      Chemical Processing Unit

Reviewed by:

Assigned to: Homicide Bureau

029

 An ASCLD/LAB Accredited Laboratory Since 1989

552

attesting person, or (B) of any foreign official whose certificate of genuineness of signature and official position relates to the execution or attestation or is in a chain of certificates of genuineness of signature and official position relating to the execution or attestation. A final certification may be made by a secretary of an embassy or legation, consul general, consul, vice consul, or consular agent of the United States, or a diplomatic or consular official of the foreign country assigned or accredited to the United States. If reasonable opportunity has been given to all parties to investigate the authenticity and accuracy of official documents, the court may, for good cause shown, order that they be treated as presumptively authentic without final certification or permit them to be evidenced by an attested summary with or without final certification.

(4) Certified copies of public records. A copy of an official record or report or entry therein, or of a document authorized by law to be recorded or filed and actually recorded or filed in a public office, including data compilations in any form, certified as correct by the custodian or other person authorized to make the certification, by certificate complying with paragraph (1), (2), or (3) of this rule or complying with any Act of Congress or rule prescribed by the Supreme Court pursuant to statutory authority.

(5) Official publications. Books, pamphlets, or other publications purporting to be issued by public authority.

(6) Newspapers and periodicals. Printed materials purporting to be newspapers or periodicals.

(7) Trade inscriptions and the like. Inscriptions, signs, tags, or labels purporting to have been affixed in the course of business and indicating ownership, control, or origin.

(8) Acknowledged documents. Documents accompanied by a certificate of acknowledgment executed in the manner provided by law by a notary public or other officer authorized by law to take acknowledgments.

(9) Commercial paper and related documents. Commercial paper, signatures thereon, and documents relating thereto to the extent provided by general commercial law.

(10) Presumptions under Acts of Congress. Any signature, document, or other matter declared by Act of Congress to be presumptively or prima facie genuine or authentic.

(11) Certified domestic records of regularly conducted activity. The original or a duplicate of a domestic record of regularly conducted activity that would be admissible under Rule 803(6) if accompanied by a written declaration of its custodian or other qualified person, in a manner complying with any Act of Congress or rule prescribed by the Supreme Court pursuant to statutory authority, certifying that the record:

(A) was made at or near the time of the occurrence of the matters set forth by, or from information transmitted by, a person with knowledge of those matters;

(B) was kept in the course of the regularly conducted activity; and

(C) was made by the regularly conducted activity as a regular practice.

A party intending to offer a record into evidence under this paragraph must provide written notice of that intention to all adverse parties, and must make the record and declaration available for inspection sufficiently in advance of their offer into evidence to provide an adverse party with a fair opportunity to challenge them.

(12) Certified foreign records of regularly conducted activity. In a civil case, the original or a duplicate of a foreign record of regularly conducted activity that would be admissible under Rule 803(6) if accompanied by a written declaration by its custodian or other qualified person certifying that the record:

(A) was made at or near the time of the occurrence of the matters set forth by, or from information transmitted by, a person with knowledge of those matters;

(B) was kept in the course of the regularly conducted activity; and

(C) was made by the regularly conducted activity as a regular practice.

The declaration must be signed in a manner that, if falsely made, would subject the maker to criminal penalty under the laws of the country where the declaration is signed. A party intending to offer a record into evidence under this paragraph must provide written notice of that intention to all adverse parties, and must make the record and declaration available for inspection sufficiently in advance of their offer into evidence to provide an adverse party with a fair opportunity to challenge them.

Fortunately, the process of authentication is streamlined for certain evidence. Under certain circumstances you need not call the government employee to testify about a public record. However in recognition of the rights of defendants and others, there are some requirements. For example, you may not be required to subpoena the government official to testify, but you do need a "certified copy." The "self-authentication" rules of 902 represent a balancing of the need for accuracy against the recognition of busy schedules and high costs (practical considerations).

Again, simply because something is deemed self-authenticating does not preclude other objections about the evidence. For example, a newspaper is self-authenticating, but that does not mean it is not hearsay.

Question

902-1   Is the birth certificate below self-authenticating?

902-2   Is the "Chemical Processing Examination Report" above self-authenticating? Would it be hearsay? Would introduction of it without the testimony of Donna Brandelli violate the Confrontation Clause?

CERTIFICATION OF VITAL RECORD

COUNTY OF LOS ANGELES • REGISTRAR-RECORDER/COUNTY CLERK

CERTIFICATE OF LIVE BIRTH
STATE OF CALIFORNIA
USE BLACK INK ONLY

19519072882

LOCAL REGISTRATION DISTRICT AND CERTIFICATE NUMBER

STATE FILE NUMBER

THIS CHILD	1A. NAME OF CHILD — FIRST (GIVEN) SALVADOR	1B. MIDDLE		1C. LAST (FAMILY) FUENTES III
	2. SEX MALE	3A. THIS BIRTH, SINGLE, TWIN, ETC. SINGLE	3B. IF MULTIPLE, THIS CHILD 1ST, 2ND, ETC. —	4A. DATE OF BIRTH — MM/DD/CCYY 06/18/1995	4B. HOUR — (24 HOUR CLOCK TIME) 0248

PLACE OF BIRTH	5A. PLACE OF BIRTH — NAME OF HOSPITAL OR FACILITY PACIFIC ALLIANCE MEDICAL NTR	5B. STREET ADDRESS — STREET, NUMBER, OR LOCATION 531 W. COLLEGE ST.	
	5C. CITY LOS ANGELES	5D. COUNTY LOS ANGELES	5E. PLANNED PLACE OF BIRTH HOSPITAL

FATHER OF CHILD	6A. NAME OF FATHER — FIRST (GIVEN) SALVADOR	6B. MIDDLE —	6C. LAST (FAMILY) FUENTES JR.	7. STATE OF BIRTH MEXICO	8. DATE OF BIRTH 07/10/67

MOTHER OF CHILD	9A. NAME OF MOTHER — FIRST (GIVEN) CONSUELO	9B. MIDDLE —	9C. LAST (MAIDEN) TELLECHEA	10. STATE OF BIRTH CA	11. DATE OF BIRTH 06/08/74

PARENT'S CERTIFICATION	I CERTIFY THAT I HAVE REVIEWED THE STATED INFORMATION AND THAT IT IS TRUE AND CORRECT TO THE BEST OF MY KNOWLEDGE.	12A. PARENT OR OTHER INFORMANT — SIGNATURE CONSUELO TELLECHEA	12B. RELATIONSHIP TO CHILD MOTHER	12C. DATE SIGNED 06/19/95
CERTIFICATION OF BIRTH	I CERTIFY THAT THE CHILD WAS BORN ALIVE AT THE DATE, HOUR AND PLACE STATED	13A. ATTENDANT OR CERTIFIER — SIGNATURE — DEGREE OR TITLE David Ling MD	13B. LICENSE NUMBER C029051	13C. DATE SIGNED 07-12-95
	13D. TYPED NAME, TITLE AND MAILING ADDRESS OF ATTENDANT D LING, MD, 17692 BEACH BL #305, HUNTINGTON BEACH		14. TYPED NAME AND TITLE OF CERTIFIER IF OTHER THAN ATTENDANT

LOCAL REGISTRAR	15A. DATE OF DEATH	15B. STATE FILE NO. (STATE USE ONLY)	16. LOCAL REGISTRAR — SIGNATURE Robert C. Gatz	17. DATE ACCEPTED FOR REGISTRATION 07/24/1995

011881

This is to certify that this document is a true copy of the official record filed with the Registrar-Recorder/County Clerk.

Conny B. McCormack

CONNY B. McCORMACK
Registrar-Recorder/County Clerk

JUL 1 6 2007

This copy not valid unless prepared on engraved border displaying the Seal and Signature of the Registrar-Recorder-County Clerk.

019450486

ARTICLE X. CONTENTS OF WRITINGS, RECORDINGS, AND PHOTOGRAPHS

Rule 1001. Definitions

For purposes of this article the following definitions are applicable:

(1) Writings and recordings. "Writings" and "recordings" consist of letters, words, or numbers, or their equivalent, set down by handwriting, typewriting, printing, Photostatting, photographing, magnetic impulse, mechanical or electronic recording, or other form of data compilation.

(2) Photographs. "Photographs" include still photographs, X-ray films, video tapes, and motion pictures.

(3) Original. An "original" of a writing or recording is the writing or recording itself or any counterpart intended to have the same effect by a person executing or issuing it. An "original" of a photograph includes the negative or any print therefrom. If data are stored in a computer or similar device, any printout or other output readable by sight, shown to reflect the data accurately, is an "original".

(4) Duplicate. A "duplicate" is a counterpart produced by the same impression as the original, or from the same matrix, or by means of photography, including enlargements and miniatures, or by mechanical or electronic re-recording, or by chemical reproduction, or by other equivalent techniques which accurately reproduces the original.

The 1000 rules are referred to as the "best evidence" rules. This often confuses students because of course they interpret the rule to require parties to introduce the very best evidence available. That is not the purpose of the rules. A better title for these rules might be "the requirement of an original if the issue in the case is the writing, recording, or photograph itself." The reach of the rule is actually quite narrow, and the rule seems to be honored more in the breach. In what instances would the content of a writing, recording, or photograph be the actual issue in a case? Consider a contract, copyright infringement, or obscenity case. The *Bright Tunes Music v. Harrisongs Music*, 420 F. Supp. 177 (S.D.N.Y. 1976) case is an example of a copyright infringement case. George Harrison, a former Beatle, was sued by the Bright Tunes Music Co. for copyright infringement. The company maintained that its song "He's So Fine" (composed by Ronald Mack and recorded by the Chiffons) was stolen by George Harrison in his song "My Sweet Lord." Harrison lost the case, although the judge found that he had not copied the song intentionally. Incidentally, Phil Spector produced the Harrison hit "My Sweet Lord." The Best Evidence Rule would apply in that case.

In most cases, the Best Evidence Rule does not apply.

Question

1001-1   Would the Best Evidence Rule be at issue in the *Spector* case?

Rule 1002. Requirement of Original

To prove the content of a writing, recording, or photograph, the original writing, recording, or photograph is required, except as otherwise provided in these rules or by Act of Congress.

Question

1002-1   Would the State be attempting to prove the content of this photograph so that an original photograph is required?

Rule 1003. Admissibility of Duplicates

A duplicate is admissible to the same extent as an original unless (1) a genuine question is raised as to the authenticity of the original or (2) in the circumstances it would be unfair to admit the duplicate in lieu of the original.

An interesting case that illustrates this rule is *Seiler v. Lucasfilm, Ltd.*, 808 F.2d 1316 (9th Cir. 1986) (reconstructions of "Garthian Striders" in a copyright infringement case).

Rule 1005. Public Records

The contents of an official record, or of a document authorized to be recorded or filed and actually recorded or filed, including data compilations in any form, if otherwise admissible, may be proved by copy, certified as correct in accordance with Rule 902 or testified to be correct by a witness who has compared it with the original. If a copy which complies with the foregoing cannot be obtained by the exercise of reasonable diligence, then other evidence of the contents may be given.

ARTICLE XI. MISCELLANEOUS RULES

Rule 1101. Applicability of Rules

(a) Courts and judges.

These rules apply to the United States district courts, the District Court of Guam, the District Court of the Virgin Islands, the District Court for the Northern Mariana Islands, the United States courts of appeals, the United States Claims Court, and to the United States bankruptcy judges and United States magistrate judges, in the actions, cases, and proceedings and to the extent hereinafter set forth. The terms "judge" and "court" in these rules include United States bankruptcy judges and United States magistrate judges.

(b) Proceedings generally.

These rules apply generally to civil actions and proceedings, including admiralty and maritime cases, to criminal cases and proceedings, to contempt proceedings except those in which the court may act summarily, and to proceedings and cases under title 11, United States Code.

(c) Rule of privilege.

The rule with respect to privileges applies at all stages of all actions, cases, and proceedings.

(d) Rules inapplicable.

The rules (other than with respect to privileges) do not apply in the following situations:

(1) *Preliminary questions of fact*. The determination of questions of fact preliminary to admissibility of evidence when the issue is to be determined by the court under Rule 104.

(2) *Grand jury*. Proceedings before grand juries.

(3) *Miscellaneous proceedings*. Proceedings for extradition or rendition; preliminary examinations in criminal cases; sentencing, or granting or revoking probation; issuance of warrants for arrest, criminal summonses, and search warrants; and proceedings with respect to release on bail or otherwise.

(e) Rules applicable in part.

In the following proceedings these rules apply to the extent that matters of evidence are not provided for in the statutes which govern procedure therein or in other rules prescribed by the Supreme Court pursuant to statutory authority: the trial of misdemeanors and other petty offenses before United States magistrate judge; review of agency actions when the facts are subject to trial de novo under section 706(2)(F) of title 5, United States Code; review of orders of the Secretary of Agriculture under section 2 of the Act entitled "An Act to authorize association of producers of agricultural products" approved February 18, 1922 (7 U.S.C. 292), and under section 6 and 7(c) of the Perishable Agricultural Commodities Act, 1930 (7 U.S.C. 499f, 499g(c)); naturalization and revocation of naturalization under sections 310-318 of the Immigration and Nationality Act (8 U.S.C. 1421-1429); prize proceedings in admiralty under sections 7651-7681 of title 10, United States Code; review of orders of the Secretary of the Interior under section 2 of the Act entitled "An Act authorizing associations of producers of aquatic

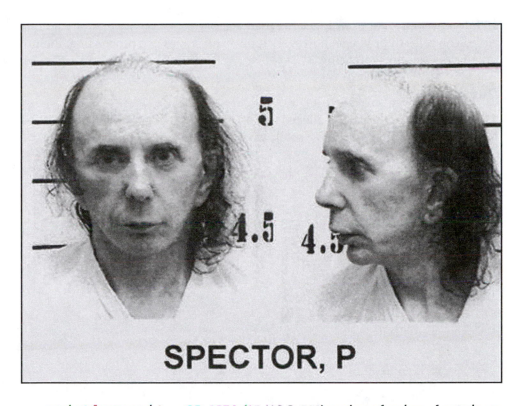

SPECTOR, P

products" approved June 25, 1934 (15 U.S.C. 522); review of orders of petroleum control boards under section 5 of the Act entitled "An act to regulate interstate and foreign commerce in petroleum and its products by prohibiting the shipment in such commerce of petroleum and its products produced in violation of State law, and for other purposes", approved February 22, 1935 (15 U.S.C. 715d); actions for fines, penalties, or forfeitures under part V of title IV of the Tariff Act of 1930 (19 U.S.C. 1581-1624), or under the Anti-Smuggling Act (19 U.S.C. 1701-1711); criminal libel for condemnation, exclusion of imports, or other proceedings under the Federal Food, Drug, and Cosmetic Act (21 U.S.C. 301-392); disputes between seamen under sections 4079, 4080, and 4081 of the Revised Statutes (22 U.S.C. 256-258); habeas corpus under sections 2241-2254 of title 28, United States Code; motions to vacate, set aside or correct sentence under section 2255 of title 28, United States Code; actions for penalties for refusal to transport destitute seamen under section 4578 of the Revised Statutes (46 U.S.C. 679); actions against the United States under the Act entitled "An Act authorizing suits against the United States in admiralty for damage caused by and salvage service rendered to public vessels belonging to the United States, and for other purposes", approved March 3, 1925 (46 U.S.C. 781-790), as implemented by section 7730 of title 10, United States Code.

The Rules (provided the Federal Rules were applicable in the *Spector* case) do not apply to Grand Jury hearings. They are inapplicable in the sentencing phase of the trials as well. Once a verdict is reached, the prohibitive Rules of 404 and

609 do not apply. All prior incidents (bad acts, arrests, convictions) are admissible. The rules of privilege, however, apply at all stages of a proceeding, including discovery and sentencing.

Question

1101-1   If one of the parties alleged that an expert was not qualified and wished to question that expert (on *voir dire*), would the rules of evidence apply?

APPENDIX A: HOW TO APPROACH EVIDENCE

Does it even fall within the Rules of Evidence? (Rules 101 and 1101)

Is it a preliminary question — and the Rules do not apply? (Rule 104)

Does the matter fall within a *privilege* (Rules 501 and 502)? Remember a privilege applies at all stages of the proceedings.

Is it **Relevant**? (Rule 401, et al.)

- If it's relevant, is it excluded for public policy reasons? (Rules 407 to 411)
- Is it subject to special rules because it's a sexual assault case? (Rules 412 to 415)

Is the witness *competent* to testify?

Is it **Character** Evidence?

- **Defendant** — 404(a) and (b) — remember the Defendant may also be a Witness. If Defendant offers — opens the door
- **Victim** — 404(b) — if Defendant offers, double door opening
- **Witness** — Rules 608 and 609
- If it is character, is it in the proper form? Rule 405 and extrinsic evidence rules
- Is it habit? Rule 406

Is this *opinion* testimony?

- Lay witness — Rule 701
- Expert witness — Rules 702 to 705

Is this a writing, recording, or photograph?

- Is the writing, recording or photograph at issue? ("**Best Evidence**" — Rules 1001 to 1006)
- Do you have the "original" or is the original excused for some reason?

Is this **Hearsay**?

- Out of court statements that are defined as "not hearsay" — Rule 801
- Does it fall within a hearsay exception (Rules 803 and 804 — under 804, declarant must be unavailable — also try 807 residual exception (dump rule))

Does the admission of the statement violate the *Confrontation Clause* of the 6th Amendment?

- Only applies in criminal cases when the statement is "testimonial"
- Has the right to confrontation been waived?

Has the evidence been properly *authenticated*?

Is the probative value SUBSTANTIALLY outweighed by the prejudicial effect? Rule 403 — but special rules in sexual assault cases.

APPENDIX B*: CONFRONTATION CLAUSE — POST-*CRAWFORD*

CRAWFORD v. WASHINGTON, 541 U.S. 36 (2004)

"Where testimonial evidence is at issue, however, the Sixth Amendment demands what the common law required: unavailability and a prior opportunity for cross-examination. We leave for another day any effort to spell out a comprehensive definition of 'testimonial.' Whatever else the term covers, it applies at a minimum to prior testimony at a preliminary hearing, before a grand jury, or at a former trial; and to police interrogations. These are the modern practices with closest kinship to the abuses at which the Confrontation Clause was directed."

APPLIES

- ▶ Criminal cases — against the accused
- ▶ Unavailable witness
- ▶ "Testimonial" — "ex parte in-court testimony or its equivalent"
- ▶ No prior opportunity to cross-examine
- ▶ Even the hearsay rules let it in (test is now divorced from hearsay analysis)
- ▶ "at a minimum" to:
  - ■ Prior testimony at a preliminary hearing
  - ■ Grand jury or former trial
  - ■ Police interrogation
  - ■ The "involvement of government officers"
- ▶ Sir Walter Raleigh-type situations
- ▶ Made under circumstance which would lead an objective witness reasonably to believe that the statement would be available for use at a later trial
- ▶ Affidavits
- ▶ Custodial examinations
- ▶ Prior testimony with no opportunity to cross-examine
- ▶ "similar pretrial statements that declarants **would reasonably expect to be used prosecutorially**"
- ▶ Depositions
- ▶ "Structured Police Questioning"
- ▶ Written statements in an affidavit to a police officer (*Hammon*)
- ▶ Possible written statements in a letter to a neighbor (*Jensen* — on appeal)

*Caution — Confrontation Clause cases are being decided at a rapid pace.

- ▶ Voicemail to a police officer
- ▶ Statement of a confidential informant (*Cromer*)
- ▶ Some 911 calls (see *Davis*)
- ▶ Lab report/drug analysis report (*Melendez-Diaz*)
- ▶ Accomplice confessions
- ▶ Statements to a nurse (if victim's condition had stabilized) (*Cannon* — Tennessee)

DOES NOT APPLY

- ▶ Civil case
- ▶ Accused offering statement
- ▶ Witness available
- ▶ Accused had a prior opportunity to cross-examine
- ▶ "Non-testimonial"
- ▶ Admission of a party opponent
- ▶ If witness is in court
- ▶ The statement is not offered for its truth (but some commentary on this)
- ▶ "Casual remark to an acquaintance"
- ▶ Statements to friends and family (*Giles*)
- ▶ Dying declaration — "on the brink of death" (*Giles*)
- ▶ 911 call (depends — see *Davis*) — if to meet an on-going emergency
- ▶ Statements to neighbors/son's teacher
- ▶ Autopsy report (*Feliz* — 2d Cir. but see *Melendez-Diaz*)
- ▶ Affidavit prepared for trial (*Ellis* — 7th Cir.)
- ▶ Excited utterance (Pursley — 10th Cir.)
- ▶ Statements made for medical diagnosis — "to receive treatment" (*Giles*, and *Santos* — 5th Cir.)
- ▶ Business record in furtherance of a conspiracy (*Giles*)
- ▶ Business records (provided that they are not prepared for use at trial) (*Melendez-Diaz*)
- ▶ Statements in furtherance of a conspiracy
- ▶ Statements made to a fellow prisoner (*Honken* — 8th Cir.)
- ▶ Immigration files (*Burgos* — 7th Cir., and five other Circuits)
- ▶ "Background information on review of tax returns (*Goosby* — 6th Cir.)
- ▶ Spontaneous statements (*Buda* — New Jersey)
- ▶ Forfeiture by misconduct — but only if the defendant meant to make the declarant unavailable to testify — not simply to make the declarant unavailable (*Giles*)
- ▶ Some jurisdictions — level of proof is clear and convincing
- ▶ Other jurisdictions — level of proof is preponderance of the evidence

APPENDIX C: CHARACTER EVIDENCE CHART

Defendant	Victim	Witness
		Remember, **Defendant** or **Victim** could also be a **Witness**
Rules 404 and 405	Rules 404 and 405	Rules 608 and 609
May ALWAYS introduce his/her own character (as long as relevant) — in a *criminal case*	Defendant in a *criminal case* may ALWAYS bring up the character of the victim (as long as it's a relevant character trait)	May not "bolster" witness — no good character until witness has been attacked
• But, if does, opens the door — prosecution may rebut with evidence on the same trait of character	• But, double door opening — that character trait of the victim as offered by the prosecution (rebuttal) AND the same character trait of the defendant	**Reputation and Opinion** — Only may refer to character for truthfulness or untruthfulness
May ALWAYS introduce a relevant character trait of the victim in a *criminal case*	• Homicide case — evidence of peaceful character trait of the victim offered by the prosecution in its case in chief — to rebut evidence that the victim was the first aggressor (e.g., self-defense cases)	**Specific Instances** — May NOT be proved by *Extrinsic Evidence* — if offered for the purpose of attacking or supporting the witness's *character or truthfulness* (but may for other credibility inquiry*)
• But, if does, double door opening — (see victim) on same trait of character		• May inquire into on cross (subject to decision of court) — if for truthfulness or untruthfulness:
Prosecution MAY NOT introduce character evidence of the defendant in a criminal case in its case in chief (unless defendant opens the door)	• May not "bolster: the victim's character (except as above — homicide case) until attacked	1) Concerning the witness's own character for truthfulness or untruthfulness; or
May NEVER use character to prove "action in conformity therewith" — propensity — except in sexual assault cases (see Rules 413, 414, and 415)	• See Rule 412 for sexual assault cases	2) Concerning the character for truthfulness or untruthfulness of another witness — as to which the witness being cross examined has testified
But, may introduce character for "another purpose" — 404(b) "prior bad	HOW TO PROVE CHARACTER — Rule 405 (same as in Defendant column)	

Defendant	Victim	Witness
acts" — such as motive, opportunity, intent, preparation, plan, knowledge, identity or absence of mistake — but on request — notice HOW TO PROVE CHARACTER — Rule 405 • Opinion and reputation — always (as long as character admissible [must get over 404 hurdle first]) • Specific instances — on cross • Specific instances — when character is an essential element of a charge, claim or defense (e.g., libel, slander, malicious prosecution, entrapment, defamation, character in a custody case		No 5th amendment waiver *See Advisory Comments for 2003 amendment to see the difference between "character for truthfulness" and "credibility" **Conviction of a Crime** For purposes of attacking the character for truthfulness of a witness — • Other than accused — felony (subject to 403) • Accused — felony (if prohibitive value outweighs the prejudicial effect) no 403 here • If crime of dishonesty or false statement (*crimen falsi*) — e.g., perjury, false statement, fraud, embezzlement, false pretense • Generally, 10-year limit • Not admissible if pardon, etc. • Juvenile convictions usually not admissible • Pendency or appeal does not make it inadmissible — but may mention appeal

APPENDIX D: HEARSAY HELPER

1. WHO IS THE DECLARANT?
2. IS IT A STATEMENT?
3. WAS THE STATEMENT MADE OUT OF COURT?
4. IS THE STATEMENT BEING USED TO *PROVE THE TRUTH OF THE MATTER ASSERTED?*

   **Is* it offered to prove the substance of its contents?

   **Is* it relevant in a manner that relies on its truthfulness?

   ▶ What is the substance of the statement?

   ▶ What is the relevant purpose for which the statement is offered?

   ▶ Is the truth or falsity of the statement irrelevant?
5. DOES THE STATEMENT QUALIFY AS "NOT HEARSAY" ACCORDING TO THE RULES OF EVIDENCE?

   ▶ Is it a "prior inconsistent statement?"

   ▶ Is there an opportunity to cross examine now?

   ▶ Was the statement given under oath?

   ▶ Is it a prior *consistent* statement now being offered to rebut?

   ▶ Is it an identification?

   ▶ Is it an ADMISSION?

   ▶ ANY prior statement of a party.

   ▶ Adoptive Admissions — 801(d)(2)(B)

   ▶ Vicarious Admissions — 801(d)(2)(C) and (D)

   ▶ Coconspirator Statements
6. IF IT IS HEARSAY, DOES IT FALL WITHIN ANY OF THE EXCEPTIONS TO THE HEARSAY RULE?

   ▶ 803 — 23 Exceptions

   ▶ 804 — 4 Exceptions — Declarant must be unavailable

   ▶ 807 — Residual Exception "Dump Rule."

APPENDIX E: SPOUSAL PRIVILEGES

Confidential Communication Privilege

- Both spouses hold the privilege — one spouse may bar another spouse from testifying
- Must be made in confidence
- Does not cover statements before or after marriage
- Confidential communications made during marriage are protected forever
- Must be a valid marriage
- Does not apply where one spouse is charged with committing a crime against the other
- Does not apply if spouse is charged with a crime against the child of either spouse

Testimonial Privilege

- Held only by the witness spouse — may elect to testify
- Not limited to confidential communications
- All subjects, including matters that occurred before marriage
- Must be a valid marriage
- Divorce, annulment, death, permanent separation — ends the privilege
- Does not apply where one spouse is charged with committing a crime against the other
- Does not apply if spouse is charged with a crime against a child of either spouse

TABLE OF CASES

INDEX